The Ultimate Golf Book

The Ultimate Golf Book

Edited by Charles McGrath and David McCormick
Historical text by John Garrity

HOUGHTON MIFFLIN COMPANY • BOSTON • NEW YORK • 2002

Copyright © 2002 by Hilltown Press
All rights reserved

For information about permission to reproduce selections from this book,
write to Permissions, Houghton Mifflin Company, 215 Park Avenue South,
New York, New York 10003.

Visit our Web site at www.houghtonmifflinbooks.com.

Library of Congress Cataloging-in-Publication Data
The ultimate golf book : a history and a celebration of the world's greatest
game / edited by Charles McGrath and David McCormick ; historical
text by John Garrity.
    p.   cm.
Includes bibliographical references and index.
ISBN 0-618-14546-X
1. Golf — History. I. McGrath, Charles. II. McCormick, David, 1961–
III. Garrity, John.
GV963 .U48 2002   796.352—dc21   2001051617

Book design by Elizabeth Johnsboen and Wendy Palitz
Photography editor: Gregory Payan

Printed in the United States of America

QWT 10 9 8 7 6 5 4 3 2 1

For the guys we play with:

Chip, Steg, Lew, Les, and Tom
and
George, Joan, Andy, Wardell, and Michael

Contents

Tiger Woods at the
2001 Masters.

The ninth at
Pebble Beach.

Greg Norman at the 1986
British Open at Turnberry.

Introduction

My regular playing partners will not be surprised to learn that I'm going to take a mully right here on the first tee. Despite what it says on the cover, this is *not* the ultimate golf book. There will be dozens more coming down the chute any minute: instruction books, rule books, etiquette books, history books, anecdote books, picture books, books about breaking 80, 90, or 100, books that heal the golfer's soul, books that offer balm to the golfer's anxious psyche, and—who knows?—maybe even books about dieting your way to a better game. They may not be as good or as inclusive as this particular

book, but if you're a golfer who likes to read, you can't have too many golf books. They're a little like golf courses: there's no such thing as a really bad one, or one that can't teach you *something*.

You don't have to be a reader to be a golfer, of course. The truly great golfers, it seems fair to say, are not bookish at all. It's hard to imagine Ben or Arnie holed up in a library somewhere. They were on the course or on the range, or they were in the shop, working on

their clubs. Ben Crenshaw, it is said, has an enviable collection of golf books, but how many has he really read? He means to get to them someday, I have no doubt, but in the meantime there's golf to be played. Crenshaw is already *good,* don't forget, and can tee it up wherever he likes. He doesn't need to pore over a manual in hopes of discovering how to fix his slice, or page through one of those glossy coffee table books — golf's equivalent of porno — dreaming of holes he'll never get to see in person.

For many of the rest of us, though, reading about golf is the next best thing to playing it. Golf books are our solace, our refuge — the place where we go to dream. It's mostly from reading that we get our "tips" — those nuggets of hopeful wisdom that are as essential to us as muscatel to a wino: arms like rope, head steady as a rock, ring the bell, swing through butter, breathe in, breathe out, hum a tune, sweep the ball, pinch the ball, don't even think about the ball, stay down, finish high. We carry these thoughts around in our heads until they lose their magic, and then we forget them and read some new tips, which are just the old tips phrased differently, but that's enough. Their temporary freshness promises transformation.

It's also through reading that we put ourselves in touch with the history of golf, which is one of the things that make this game special and rewarding. John Stark, a Scottish pro whom you'll meet later on in this book, believes that no golfer should be allowed to step on a course unless he or she can pass an exam in basic golf history. That may be a little extreme, but those of us who know some golf history know that it is its own reward. It makes golf—even our own ordinary, unhistoric golf—more fun.

History is the spine of this book. We asked John Garrity to tell the old story yet again: Old Tom and Young Tom. Francis Ouimet. Gene Sarazen and the double eagle. Bobby and Ben. Babe and Betsy. Arnie and Jack. Tiger. Hickory shafts and featheries, graphite and solid core. St. Andrews. Augusta. Oakmont. Pebble Beach. We know this stuff by heart and yet we can never hear it too often, especially when the story is told, as John has told it here, with a lively and irreverent point of view.

Reading about golf also puts us in touch with all the other people fortunate enough to play it—pros and hackers alike. Even when you play by yourself, golf is a communal activity, one that's enhanced by sharing and remembering. So in putting together the rest of the book, we called up some of our favorite writers—golf writers, that is, and also writers who happen to golf—and begged them to contribute. In most cases it didn't take much arm-twisting.

We knew there were certain subjects and personalities that had to be covered. How could you have an ultimate golf book without a piece about Tiger or Hogan? It would be nice, we decided, if we could do something on golf course architecture, and maybe pay tribute to some of the old-timers. So there was a certain amount of lobbying, but for the most part we let the writers write what they wanted, which in most cases was something about their personal connection to the game. The result, we hope, is sort of like sitting on the clubhouse porch in late afternoon, cold one in hand, and listening to one great golf yarn after another.

That, too, is part of what makes golf special—the stories we tell.

The game itself is a kind of narrative. We set off, full of hope and expectation, we encounter difficulties and reversals, our character is tested, our spirits soar and plummet, and then we head for home, where, with relief or sadness, or maybe both, we rap the final putt into its hole. Then, as soon as we're done, we play it all over again in our heads, and it gets better and better in the telling and retelling. This may be why golf appeals to so many writers—because, as Ward Just suggests in his essay here, golf seems at some level to soothe and refresh the writerly mind. It's also the perfect writer's distraction: you can play a round and tell yourself that you're subconsciously working on your book at the same time.

The small-ball theory of sportswriting has by now been mostly discredited—the theory that holds that the quality of a game's literature is inversely proportional to the size of the ball that game employs. This, if you believe the theorists, is why there are more good baseball writers than bowling writers. But then where are the Ping-Pong scribes, and shouldn't there be classic works on marbles? In truth, good writing is good writing. Rick Reilly, one of our contributors, writes with equal skill about golf and every other game played with a ball, and even those that employ no ball at all. If golf and baseball have any advantage over the other sports, it's only that they take place more slowly and allow the harried scribe a chance to collect his thoughts and take a few notes.

But golf, unlike baseball, has the additional advantage of being a game we can still play as well as watch. Our connection is deeper, more personal, and sooner or later this game, so difficult and yet so satisfying, brings out the poet, as well as the cynic and the ironist, in all of us. It's a game that somehow asks to be celebrated in words as well as in deeds and pictures, and that's what we've tried to do here—to give some sense of golf's range and possibilities, and a reminder of how many and varied its pleasures are.

Lucky Us

BY RICK REILLY

Lucky you. You were born in the time of Tiger Woods. You were alive when the single most dominating athlete of our age was at his pupil-dilating best. Take a look at him. No, *really* look at him.

Six-foot-two. One hundred eighty pounds. Cut. Size thirty-two waist. Ripped forearms. Half-miler's legs. Works out two hours a day. Every day. Tattooless. Long fingers that tend to fist up. A white strip of tape on the middle finger of his right hand that once protected a split in his skin. Now there for superstition.

Size nine and a half feet. Scratchy throat, allergic to everything green. Runny nose. Watery, Lasixed eyes. Pepsodent smile. An overbite. Smallish, unpierced ears. Sleepy lids over a hitman's stare. Fade haircut. High sideburns. Receding hairline, just like Pop's.

Whites and blacks and reds. Clothes picked out by Nike a year before, to coordinate with product introductions. Aren't yours? Tiger wears a blue-striped shirt, your pharmacist wants to wear a blue-striped shirt. Top button fastened. Sleeves loose and just over the elbow, except the left one, which is constantly being hitched up two inches, before shots, after shots, even in press conferences. Shirt bloused a half-inch over designer belt. Cuffed pants. Everything ironed himself.

A spy's mind. Won't talk about his workouts. Won't talk about his girlfriends. Won't compare eras. Doesn't like his caddie to talk to the press. (See: Fluff.) Won't guess, hypothesize, or speculate. Rarely gives one-on-ones. Rarely gives ten-on-ones. When the car comes to get him, always has to drive. Always has to win, be it Ping-Pong or Mortal Kombat.

Aw-shucks all press conferences. Nah, he just "whiffs" it out there 340 feet. He "wiggles" in the 20-footer. He "half-chunks" it in the jar. Has said 4,032 times: "Well, broke 80 today, so that's good." Been on national television since he was two. Done more press conferences than all Bushes put together. Never bites. Never gives in. Never lets you all the way through. "You thinking of history tonight?" we ask him on the eve of the Tiger Slam, April 2001. "Nah," he says. "I'm thinking of my swing."

A true golf geek. All golf. All the time. Known in college as Erkel. A dreadful dancer. A-plus student. Don't want grades messing with golf. Had to have his homework done before he could play golf, so he'd do it a day ahead of time. Good with women, but not within a par five of committing. Don't want women messing with golf. Currently in a torrid affair with his lob wedge.

The most watched golfer in history. Surrounded. Choppers and blimps, police escorts and 600-millimeter lenses and multitudes and yet the even pace of a monk. "It is calm in the eye of the hurricane," explains his mother, Tida. An unbreakable way. A zen-like, world-shunning focus, but a zen-like, world-seeing awareness. Did you feel that? The slightest stir of a leaf or breath of wind on the neck? He does.

Fifteenth hole. Sunday, 2001 Masters. Top of the backswing. Loaded like a catapult. All systems go. The downswing begins to explode. Forty feet away, a disposable camera clicks. He stops, all systems off. Like Niagara freezing halfway down. A glare that would melt titanium. A trick his pop, the old Kansas State catcher, taught him. Son could do it with a golf club. Pop could do it with a baseball bat. Regroup. Re-routine. Bust it right down the middle. You get trained by Lieutenant Colonel Earl Woods, an Army psychological warfare expert, it's no problem.

A tee with his name on it. A Nike Tour Accuracy TW ball with TIGER printed on both sides. That ball placed on the tee so the swoosh is centered on the face of the club at address. One smoosh with the right foot behind the ball. Two practice swings behind it. A stare into the shot to come. Wait. One, two seconds. Now set the right foot in place, now the left. Two waggles, club hovering. Count one, two, and the club sweeps straight back, left shoulder under chin, club to three-quarter, knee bent and locked. A cat's whisker of a pause, a furious uncoil, 122 miles per hour at impact, a chilling clap of noise, right shoulder under the chin (his shirts used to wear out there), then up and through, unblinking, mouth closed, following the flight of another ozone-depleter.

Stuff the club back in a bag of tricks like no other. The tiger head cover with "Love from Mom" stitched in white in Thai. An aardvark on the Titleist 970 three-wood. Titanium Titleist 975D driver (7.5-degree loft), Titleist forged irons copied spec for spec off Mizunos. Titleist prototype pitching wedge. Volkey-designed sand and lob wedges. No one-iron.

The best driver in history. The best short game since Paul Runyan. The most skilled player ever. An eight-iron 180 yards. A driver 350. At the eighteenth at Augusta, last day, a driver 327. Uphill. To win. At Disney once, a 325-yard three-wood over water, in a win. In Canada, on the seventy-second hole, a 215-yard six-iron out of a bunker, over water, to win.

Shots Nicklaus never dreamed of. Talk of "wanting a one-yard draw there" with the driver, and actually getting it. A wind-cheating three-wood "stinger" Hogan taught to Claude Harmon, who taught it to Butch Harmon, who taught it to Tiger, who can hit it under a parked 1957 Buick 200 yards away. The big high "sweeper" hook that starts out on one side of the range and ends on the other. The dead-hands, all-arm 80-yard wedges that land and stop dead without spin. The six-iron that spins back as if it just came torquing out of a twister.

An ability to hit a pitched golf ball out of the air 200 yards. An ability to hit a rolled golf ball 250. An ability to hit two out of ten on the fly into a beer cooler 90 yards away. The Harmon school of Flying Wallenda wedge shots: skipper, spinner, skid-and-skipper, purposely toed bunker blast that comes down soft as a kitten, purposely skulled wedge out of the lip of a bunker that nestles up to six inches. Three-wood chip off the green that sets off a landslide of clubs built only for that purpose. Flop shots hit out of a silo.

A Scotty Cameron putter forged by God Himself. Reads his own putts, thanks. Each gets all four sides stalked. Then another look from behind. The hands shading the eyes for focus. As if he *needs* more focus. The wristless stroke, back and through. The absolutely motionless head, even when the putt is six feet, outside the hole, to tie for the PGA Championship. It's away. No peek. It's long since away. Still no peek. It's three-quarters to the hole. Now a peek. It's on line. Chase it down, walk it home, point. And then, as always, the

pump. Same movement. Every time. The fist stopped halfway into an uppercut. The yelling that can't be heard in an ocean of yelling. The charge to the next hole. The best clutch putter since Jack Nicklaus.

The man on the bag: Steve Williams, thirty-six. Greg Norman's and Ray Floyd's ex. New Zealand stock car racer. Not exactly Fluff. Six-four, two hundred. Flips the bag around as if it's Shirley Temple's purse. High school dropout. Caddy since fifteen. First caddy in history to win all four majors, lifetime. Has his own foundation. You would, too. Figuring 10 percent for wins, 7 percent for all other finishes, plus fees, has probably banked $4 million on the kid so far.

His boss: first in the world rankings, 19 points ahead of second. Nineteen points behind second is . . . nobody. The list only has 1,200 names. Mathematically, it's McGwire 150, Sosa 60. For 2000, first in scoring, greens in regulation, eagles, birdie leaders, total driving, money, par breakers, par-four birdie leaders, par-five birdie leaders, birdie conversions, all-around, and *Didju-see-that!?!*s.

Great masters' jaws hitting their chests. "I watch him," says Tom Watson. "I learn from him." The swing sequence Watson wants his son to put up on his wall? Woods's, not Dad's. "He's not having to beat Trevino and Player," say the old guys in the press tent. True. But if he didn't exist, wouldn't Els be Player by now? Wouldn't Mickelson be Trevino? Exquisitely fine players reduced to the horses behind Secretariat.

The holder of every major trophy and the scoring record in every major and the margin-of-victory record in every major except the PGA since 1900. Yikes! The Tiger Slam. Four tournaments, never defeated: 561–0. No Jack Fleck upset. No Orvill Moody upset. No Bob May upset. Four tournaments, closest man to him: Ernie Els: 55 shots behind. Over there, head down, David Duval. His 14-under at the 2001 Masters would've won fifty-nine of sixty-five Masters and put him in a playoff twice. The Unlucky Sperm Club. Karl Malone to Tiger's Jordan. Avis to his Hertz.

Only twenty-five. Twenty-five seasons to go. Lucky us.

chapter 1

Scotland

G olf began in the dark—in a hole actually. Some dissipated characters in medieval Scotland were out on the dunes one afternoon with their *het kolvin* sticks, slapping a ball around. One of them aimed at a rabbit burrow or a sand-filled crevice. When the ball toppled in, golf was born.

Golf historians are equally in the dark. Looking for a link to the stick-and-ball games of continental Europe, they pore over Flemish woodcuttings and sketches by Rembrandt of men in wide-brimmed hats using a bladed stick to roll a ball the size of a melon across a courtyard. Researchers are similarly enchanted by the French game of *jeu de mal,* which employed a flexible wooden

THE OLD SOD: "Hard by, in the fields called the Links, the citizens of Edinburgh divert themselves at a game called Golf in which they use a curious kind of bat tipped with horn, and small elastic balls of leather, stuffed with feathers . . ." —Tobias Smollet, 1771, *The Expedition of Humphrey Clinker.*

mallet and a wooden ball, and by the Belgian game of *chole,* in which teams of players hit wooden balls through a designated door or gate up to a mile away. (The Dutch word *tuitje,* for the small mound of earth upon which the ball was placed for the first stroke, is an obvious forerunner to the golfer's "tee.") Masters of the obvious have pointed out that a Low Countries variant of chole, called *colf,* was played in the shade of windmills as early as the thirteenth century.

Here we have a case where the lexicographer trumps the historian. The *Oxford English Dictionary* defines golf as "a game of considerable antiquity . . . in which a small hard ball is struck with various clubs into a series of small cylindrical holes made at intervals usually of a hundred yards or more . . . with the fewest possible strokes." No one reading this definition can miss what separates golf from all the other games employing clubs or mallets and small hard balls. It's that little dark place where the ball goes.

Once we accept that golf is about holes in the ground, we can reflect on the fact that the holes are dispersed over a vast natural terrain. For that we owe King David I of Scotland, a twelfth-century monarch whose idea of a good time was cathedral building. It was on David's watch that the previously forgettable fishing village of St. Andrews, on the North Sea between the Eden estuary and the River Forth, became the ecclesiastical center of Scotland. As a sop to the local folk — a hodgepodge of Picts, Celts, and assorted Norsemen — David decreed that certain lands be set aside for the free use of ordinary people. These commons or greens included some worthless tracts of "linksland" — places where rivers meet the sea, producing a rugged dunescape of sand and wild grasses. Neither David nor the common folk foresaw a recreational use for these lands—or knew, for that matter, what "recreation" was. The linksland was simply a place where any Angus or Owen could set snares in the dunes, hoping to capture a rabbit for the dinner pot.

Nevertheless, King David's decree established a pattern of land use that allowed for the development of golf, first at St. Andrews—where in 1552 Archbishop Hamilton affirmed the right of all to use the links for "golff, futball, schuteing [and] all other man-ner of pastime"—and later in the lowland shires along the Clyde and Forth estuaries. It would also give the Scots about 750 years to perfect the game before the rest of the world took notice.

What the Scots came up with was a sport that requires minimal exertion and no physical risk but demands that the players police their own conduct to a degree unknown in most other games—or in life, for that matter—while enduring whatever discomforts nature dispenses in the form of wind, rain, heat, or cold. We need only glance at the first thirteen rules of golf, set down by the Honourable Company of Edinburgh Golfers in 1774, to see how golf answers the Calvinist demand for sufferance in the face of sustained ill fortune. "If you should lose your ball by its being taken up or any other way," reads rule eight, "you are to go back to the spot where you struck last and drop another ball and allow your adversary a stroke for the misfortune." Rule eleven imagines an even more dire cir-cumstance: "If you draw your club in order to strike and proceed so far with your stroke as to be bringing down your club, if then your club should break in any way, it is to be accounted a stroke."

The game's gloomy rules owe in part to Scotland's national temper, which was formed through centuries of gory conflict with its neighbor

15.—A STYMIE.

—"DUFFERS YET." lips to give us Nerve."

—PROFESSOR TAIT. Theory of Golf.

to the south, England. James IV of Scotland, who died in 1513 at the battle of Flodden Field, was a casual golfer. His granddaughter Mary, Queen of Scots, celebrated the violent murder of her estranged husband, Lord Darnley, by playing golf at Seton with the Earl of Bothwell, the man suspected of arranging Darnley's death — and then, some years later, Mary herself lost her head at the order of her cousin Queen Elizabeth I of England. Thankfully, by the seventeenth century the crowns of England and Scotland were unified under the Stuarts, and golf temporarily replaced war and the executioner's axe as the arbiters of aristocratic disputes. The Duke of York settled a quarrel with two English noblemen in the 1680s by challenging them to a money match on the links at Leith, and like many a hustler after him, the duke showed up with a suspiciously talented partner: a shoemaker with a good swing and a sure putting stroke. The shoemaker, John Patterson, earned enough from the match to build a home in Edinburgh that stood for almost three hundred years.

As durable as Patterson's house is the concept that allowed a duke to partner with a shoemaker in the first place. The Scots developed the idea that golfers constitute a society separate from their stations in ordinary life. A king, although sovereign in the realm, could play golf with

and respect a tradesman. The tradesman, in turn, could gather with gentlemen of like interest to form a golfing society or club. The first of these societies, the Honourable Company of Edinburgh Golfers, organized itself at Leith Links around 1744, and a similar group formed at St. Andrews a decade later.

FOR THE RECORD:
St. Andrews's harbor from the early 1800s. Below: *Golf*, the oldest golf magazine, which was first published in 1890. In 1899 it became *Golf Illustrated*.

Neither club owned a golf course—the common land still belonged to all—but the clubs staged competitions and other group endeavors. The pattern was set in 1744 when the town council of Edinburgh offered a trophy in the form of a silver club; the winner of the annual competition at the Leith Links assumed the title of "Captain of Golf." St. Andrews adopted the Honourable Company's rules and took the club competition a step further by awarding each year's winner a silver golf ball, which was then attached to the silver club. With time, the silver balls hung in grapelike clusters, leading to a curious ceremony called "kissing the captain's balls."

The golfers who were the first to gain royal sanction came, however, from neither Edinburgh nor St. Andrews; for reasons known only to King William IV, that honor went, in 1833, to the upstart Perth Golfing Society, established only since 1824. The Golf Club of St. Andrews promptly petitioned the king, pointing out that the Perth golfers were relative pups. William, it is assumed, rolled his eyes and sighed, but a year later he granted his St. Andrews subjects the

TOM AND TOMMY: In the first eight years of the Open, Old Tom Morris (facing) won four of them against his rival Willie Park. In 1868, when he was just seventeen, Young Tom (below) won the Open, dethroning his father as champion—one record unlikely to be broken.

right to call themselves the Royal & Ancient Golf Club of St. Andrews. Almost two centuries later, the men's-only R&A stages the Open Championship and serves as the rules-making body for all golfers outside North America.

Although it is accurate to call golf a Scottish invention, very few Scots actually played it. Working people had no time for games, and golf balls were prohibitively expensive. Perhaps thirty golfers were playing regularly at St. Andrews at the beginning of the nineteenth century, and even smaller societies clung to life in Edinburgh, Perth, and Ayr, and in England at Blackheath. To grow, the game required a fundamental shift in economics. It needed a leisure class.

The Industrial Revolution provided that class. Up to the 1800s, goods in Europe were manufactured at the cottage level, with entire families contributing to the production of flatware, china, and woolens. The mechanization and specialization of the nineteenth century changed that system, and tradesmen found themselves able to delegate some of their work. As the textile bosses, crystal makers, and bankers took time off for recreation and networking, the ranks of golfers swelled. They, in turn, supported a growing number of golf professionals — club makers, ball makers, and greenskeepers who lived solely off the game.

The most notable of these professionals was Allan Robertson of St. Andrews. Robertson, the son of a caddie, made "feathery" balls in his kitchen with the aid of a young apprentice named Tom Morris. Robertson was also the best golfer of his time. He was the first player to break 80 at St. Andrews, and he and Morris beat all comers in a series of high-stakes foursome matches. "His style was neat and effective," the memoirist James Balfour wrote of Robertson. "His clubs were light and his stroke an easy, swift switch." The friendship between Robertson and Morris dissolved, however, when the older man caught his

St. Andrews, circa 1890,
with Old Tom near the
Swilcan Bridge.

former apprentice playing with one of the new gutta-percha golf balls, introduced in 1848. (The rubbery "gutty" was more durable and much cheaper than the feathery, and Robertson feared that it would destroy his business.) Robertson died of jaundice in 1859, at age forty-four, having reluctantly switched to the gutty himself. Morris, meanwhile, moved to Prestwick, south of Glasgow, where he designed a new twelve-hole course and served as professional and greenskeeper.

It was at Prestwick that the foundation of modern tournament golf was laid. On October 17, 1860, Morris and seven other professionals played three rounds, or thirty-six holes, for a "chal-

lenge belt" of red morocco leather and silver. The winner was the whiskered Willie Park Sr. of Musselburgh, who edged Morris by two strokes. A year later, the Prestwick Golf Club responded to the complaints of excluded amateurs by declaring the belt competition "open to all the world." This time Morris was the best of a twelve-man field, beating Park's 1860 score by eleven strokes to claim the first Open Championship. Morris would win the Open again in '62, '64, and '67, but he was soon overtaken by his own son, Tom Morris Jr., a golf prodigy. Young Tom, whose wrists were so strong that he was supposed to have snapped hickory shafts simply by waggling the club, won the

1868 Open when he was seventeen. He then went on to win the next three, claiming permanent ownership of the championship belt and first possession of the silver claret jug, the Open trophy since 1877. Sadly, Young Tom proved to be, in the modern phrase, a candle in the wind. His wife died in childbirth in 1875, and the baby was lost as well. Three months later, on Christmas morning, Young Tom was found dead in his bed in his St. Andrews home, the victim of a lung aneurysm. Today a monument in the graveyard of St. Andrews Cathedral shows him addressing a golf ball, his coat buttoned up against the gale, a Scots bonnet on his head. Forever twenty-four.

Old Tom, on the other hand, lived into the twentieth century and helped consolidate the gains that golf had made in the Victorian era. As greenskeeper at St. Andrews and professional to the R&A, Morris lived above his own golf shop, just a few feet from the eighteenth green on the Old Course. Always in demand as a designer, he traveled Scotland by donkey cart, rail, and steamer to lay out golf courses for clubs and town councils. Two of his courses—Muirfield and Prestwick—became British Open venues. Morris would also gain credit for devising the modern loop system of two nines going out from and returning to the clubhouse—a scheme designed to make the player adjust to different wind conditions.

You could argue that Tom Morris did the mop-up work on the

FOREVER YOUNG: After his third victory in 1870, Young Tom received the Open championship belt for keeps. But grief over the death of his wife killed him a few years later. Below: a long putt in a match at the Brough Golf Club in 1912.

edifice of golf. In his lifetime, the golf course assumed its modern form of eighteen holes with man-made hazards, mowed fairways, watered greens, and strategic playing options. The golf ball evolved from a fragile feather bag to a durable, dimpled sphere that could be driven long distances and spun for control. Club making entered the iron age as "cleekmakers" created an arsenal of mashies, niblicks, and rut irons capable of handling practically any lie. The Open Championship was launched and stroke play adopted as the preferred format for deciding major championships. All these developments, if one needs reminding, took place in Scotland. By 1888 there were roughly seventy courses on the old sod, with simple links blooming on the springy *machair* of the Western Isles and very bad courses emerging on the denser, fecund soils of the Highlands and lake regions.

Meanwhile, the hole — the be-all and end-all of golf — sought its own sublime exactitude. For hundreds of years, the size of the cavity had been arbitrary, ranging from three inches to more than five inches in diameter. (At the Old Course, the hole reportedly matched the diameter of a standard St. Andrews drainpipe.) The hole's depth was even less constant. When a golfer was ready to play his first shot to a new hole, he put his hand in the hole he had just putted into and took a pinch of sand upon which to tee his ball. "It often happened," the two-time British Amateur champion Horace G. Hutchinson reported with comic gravity, "that one had to lie down so as to stretch one's arm at full length in order to reach the ball at the bottom of the hole."

It was not until the nineteenth century that the Scots invented a device to cut uniform holes — either at Musselburgh in

1829 or at Royal Aberdeen in 1849, depending on which golf historian you believe. In 1874 the Crail Golf Club introduced the metal liner, which kept the hole from collapsing and rewarded the player with a pleasing rattle when his ball fell into the cup. In 1891 the R&A finally proclaimed, with a confident authority reminiscent of the old monarchs, that the hole would henceforth be "4¼ inches in diameter and at least 4 inches deep."

These dimensions, of course, made for a hole that was too small. Putting became disproportionately important, and fear and anxiety were validated as elements of the game. At the 1889 Open Championship at Musselburgh, for example, Andrew Kirkaldy made a careless back-handed swipe at his ball, poised on the edge of the fourteenth hole, and missed it entirely. "Did you try to putt that ball, Andra?" a tournament official asked. Kirkaldy replied, "Yes, and if the hole was big enough, I'd bury myself in it." The next day he lost the Open to Willie Park Jr. in an eighteen-hole playoff.

As events would soon prove, it was not just Kirkaldy's ball that hung on the brink. Within thirty years, the Scots would see their curious game spread like a benign virus to North America and beyond, and they would see it change, in the words of the American golf writer Herbert Warren Wind, "from an occult Scottish passion into a universal pastime pursued wherever grass sprouts, and sometimes where it doesn't."

The dark ages, in other words, were over.

A LADIES' FIRST: Lady Margaret Scott, second from left, won the first three British Ladies' Championships. After the third at Portrush in 1895, she retired from competitive golf. Her full-bodied swing was ahead of its time.

The Machrie Golf Club in
Islay, Scotland.

The Voice of Golf

BY VERLYN KLINKENBORG

Golf has had no greater writer than Bernard Darwin, who was born in 1876 and died in 1961. For Darwin, the golden age of golf meant "the last few years of the gutty-ball era and perhaps, though golf would have been better if it had never been invented, the first few of the rubber-cored era," which began in 1902 when the Haskell ball was introduced. In those years, the English and the Scots still dominated golf, and British golf was dominated by the Triumvirate—J. H. Taylor, Harry Vardon, and James Braid. There were many glories to come in Darwin's long life, including Jones, Hagen, Nelson, Sarazen, Hogan, and even Palmer and Nicklaus. There were the remarkable occasions when Darwin, at ages forty-five and forty-six, found himself playing, and playing well, in the heat of international competition—in the 1921 British Amateur Open and, as a competitor in a tournament he had come to cover as a journalist, in the 1922 Walker Cup.

But even during the heyday of the Triumvirate, when he was still a young man, something had already begun to pass in Darwin's life. Of the coming of the Haskell ball, he later wrote, "Some virtue had gone out of the game for ever, but it was a pleasanter and easier game, and what will ever deter mankind from pleasant paths and short cuts?" When he wrote about figures like Taylor and Vardon and Braid, he was also remembering the great golfers who preceded them. He was remembering a golf that is now unspeakably distant.

The memory of golf is both tactile and visual. You may be able to recite the accomplishments of those ancient golfers by the book, but their living swings have vanished and with them much of the essential meaning of their game. Take Darwin himself. More than any other person in the first half of the twentieth century, he is the written voice of golf. For forty-six years, he was the golf correspondent of the *London Times* and an unfailingly regular weekly essayist for *Country Life*. He fashioned prose as balanced and as pure as that of anyone who has ever written about sport, or almost anything else for that matter. The cadence of his writing might seem to tell us something about the cadence of his swing.

Consider this passage from his essay on practice in an instructional anthology called *The Game of Golf:*

> I think not only of quiet corners of many
> courses, but of many fields where the grass
> was so long that almost every stroke involved
> a search; I think of a mountain top in Wales
> and a plain in Macedonia; of innumerable
> floors on which I have tried to hit the table
> legs; I recall rain and wind and mud and the
> shades of evening falling, so that the lights
> came twinkling out in the houses round the
> links, and the ball's destiny was a matter of
> pure conjecture.

And now consider a photograph of Darwin at Aberdovey, his beloved Welsh course. The photo captures him in full coil, playing out of the thatch with a wooden-headed club. Several things suggest the aggressiveness and the choleric quality of this swing: the flying right elbow, which threatens to dislocate the arm and shoulder it's attached to, the tremendous, quivering overreach of the backswing, in which the club looks like it's dowsing for water on its own. But what really conveys Darwin's wrathful stroke is his lower body. His hips and legs look like those of a hockey player banking hard out of a turn. Darwin plans to persecute this ball—a Haskell, no doubt.

Yet both of these images—the lights twinkling at dusk beyond the edge of the golf course and the fierce man fiercely playing his way home before darkness falls—are Darwin. His subject is eternal combat in a pastoral setting, the collision of titans—and the titanic crash of self—in a green and glorious land. Like the whole brood of Darwins, including his grandfather, Charles, Darwin was a most unmilitary man. But you would never know it by the way he writes about golf. His verbs are never at parade rest. After Vardon went to America, Darwin writes, "he never mowed down his enemies in quite the same way again." When Darwin, at age eighty-one, considers the pleasures of having given up the game, he confesses, "No fatal shot, no insanely bad piece of judgment will haunt your pillow, while your undeserving conqueror goes on from round to round, goes on to the semi-final where you ought to have been."

In his autobiography, Darwin lists a few of the things he would do if he had his golfing life to live over again. His first resolution is "to make a desperate effort not to get cross." The desperateness is amusing in itself. But it also reveals the mood in which Darwin played and often wrote about the game, a mood that allowed him to understand, from inside, the psychology of born competitors. "I think that not to mind about how one plays," he writes, "is a rather anemic state, such as makes a game hardly worth the playing. Doubtless one ought not to mind losing the match if one has played one's game and there are people who say they do not, but except in a very few cases I am not quite sure that I believe them . . . If one is born a minder I think one will mind to the day of one's death." Darwin died minding.

This fervor, which sometimes broke out on the course, though never in print, in a form of golfing apoplexy, is the measure of Darwin's devotion to golf. More than once, he tried to appraise the way the game as he knew it differed from the one he saw being played around him in his old age. Many of the changes were obvious—the shift from hickory shafts to steel, from gutta-percha balls to Haskells and their modern successors, the introduction of sand wedges. To this list, Darwin would certainly have added the Americanization of the sport, especially the American zeal for practicing. There was also virtually no golf writing when he was a young man. Columnists and experts "had not discovered the subtle art of flattering the eighteen handicap golfer. The patent-never-leaving-off-golf-article-writing-steam-engine had not yet begun to work."

Yet as you read Darwin, you realize that the greatest difference in the game since his golden age is intimacy. There had been a golf boom in the 1880s, Darwin writes, but even after that boom, "to see another man with clubs in the railway carriage rack was inevitably to fall into conversation, whereas today his clubs mean no more than his umbrella, unless indeed we are afraid he may talk golf to us." The "today" in that sentence is 1952. When he writes about matches—

even casual ones—Darwin indulges in the honorific fullness of the contestants' names. After a while, it dawns on the twenty-first-century American reader that Darwin is careful with these names because their owners were almost certainly known to everyone who was likely to be reading him.

But to conclude, somehow, from that sense of intimacy that Darwin was a snob is a serious mistake. His grandfather, Charles, and his great-great-grand-father, Erasmus, were renowned men, but that was far less important to Darwin than the sheer number and variety of uncles on both sides of the family and the warmth of his maternal grandmother, Mary Anne Ruck, who lived in a "tiny grey house" called Pantlludw in Merioneth. That corner of Wales was one of the many places where Darwin felt perfectly at home, a quality that defines his character as surely as the venom he felt when being beaten in match play. He inhabits an almost perfectly defined universe, a place regulated entirely to his tastes.

We're lucky, after all, that we share with Darwin the great language of golf. The vocabulary has changed somewhat, and so has the syntax. Darwin's swing lies on the yonder side of a line dividing past from present, but not his enthusiasm for the game. Herbert Warren Wind, the great golf correspondent for *The New Yorker,* once wrote that "it is difficult to picture Bernard Darwin careening down a fairway at the wheel of a golf cart." And as the popularity of competitive match play dwindled, there was, for Darwin, less and less to love about professional golf, filled as it is, then and now, with "those dreary tournaments, 72 holes of score play, round and round and round again . . . of such unutterable slowness as to tire the sun with putting." Yet one can still go to Darwin to understand even Tiger Woods, though Darwin called him Harry Vardon. "For a little while there were two classes of people who hit a golf ball, in the one Vardon, and in the other all the other golfers. Nature enforced her invariable law; the others had to hunt Vardon and they drew closer to him, closer than ever they could have believed possible if he had not stretched them on the rack and dragged the golf out of them."

There is no leaving the subject of Bernard Darwin without a word or two about Charles Dickens. Darwin loved *Pickwick Papers* above all the other novels and, in fact, above all other literature. Like G. K. Chesterton, he was one of those rare readers who see far deeper, and with affectionate dispassion, into the heart of Dickens than the rest of us can. The result is that Darwin's prose is peopled with fictional characters and their utterances, the majority of them drawn from Dickens. Darwin drew no overt analogy between Dickens and the game of golf, but it exists nonetheless. "There is nothing to say," he says about Dickens, though he might be talking about golf itself, "except that magic is uncontrollable stuff, that it will come breaking in, and that nobody, least of all perhaps the magician himself, knows how or when it is going to do it."

Let me end, at last, with Darwin at his best, on the course, describing the final moments of the 1899 Amateur Championship at Prestwick, between John Ball and Freddie Tait, not long before they went to what Darwin calls the "South African War." The match went up and down, nip and tuck. "Grotesque hooks" were hit, and once Ball had to hit from the "hard wet sand." Finally, all tied, the two men came to the thirty-seventh hole of the day. This is how Darwin finishes. What you hear is both a mythic coda and the subtle intimation of the author's presence at the final moment, Darwin's own magic breaking in. "Finally," he writes, "as all the world knows, John Ball holed a putt, not an enormous putt but a very, very good one, perhaps 8 feet, perhaps 10, for a three at the 37th. From between somebody's legs I believe I saw him strike the ball, but I only heard it go in."

Playing with
better players

BY JOHN UPDIKE

Unhappy golfers are unhappy in their own way, but it is not true, as Tolstoy's well-known formulation would have it, that all happy golfers are alike. Some, as we see on television, have flowing, picture-book swings, and others, especially among the seniors, swat at the ball, out of short and choppy backswings. Arnold Palmer leaves his club out in front of him like a rifle, Trevino seems to be trying to slap his drive through the right side of the in-field, and Jim Furyk, a commentator has said, looks like an octopus falling out of a tree. But all seem to get the job done, or got it done in their prime, and the mystery of how lingers somewhere out of the range of TV cameras. A viewer sees the ball vanish off the right of the screen like a banana slice and hears the commentator excitedly bleat that the shot is bending in, on top of the flagstick.

No, being there in three dimensions is the only way to see for yourself, and for that reason a mediocre golfer needs now and then to play with better golfers. They show up in club tournaments or as the brother-in-law of a customary partner; they can be college students or company salesmen or vagabond scions of a snake-oil fortune. Their togs are color-coordinated; the pockets of their bags bulge with towels, rain-suits, and spare gloves. As they take practice swings on the first tee, the swish of their clubs has a higher pitch than you hear in your usual, companiably inept foursome.

Without seeming to strain, they generate club-head speed where it counts, at the bottom of the swing, where the ball is. Doesn't everybody? No: the virtually universal tendency of duffers is to hit from the top, expending wrist-cock in the first ninety degrees of the arc and thus arriving at the ball club late and weak, giving it an armsy, decelerating hit that makes the fingers tingle and digs a deadening divot on the wrong side of the ball. With that little white orb sitting up on tee or turf begging to be spanked, our lunging into the downswing as swiftly and passionately as possible makes good sense to the warrior within us — look out! the other fellow has a broadsword too!! — but couldn't be more counterproductive. The good player waits that heartbeat for the club to swing itself, and his grip shows no white knuckles; the club adheres to his hands of its own sweet will. *Swish swish:* a new beast has been released, there on the first tee.

Watching your accustomed friends set up, waggle, and attack the ball, you are conscious of their bodies as a collection of separate units struggling to get together. The arms go back as far as they conveniently can, and then fear of failure, of generating insufficient distance, pushes them up some more inches, tipping the shoulders into a reverse pivot and making the feet fight like Tinkerbell's to keep contact with the earth. The knees gyrate in agitation, and the head bobs as if signaling assent to the hopelessness of it all. First the right leg locks straight as a stick, and then the left. It is all too much activity to squeeze into two seconds; the swing circumscribes a roughly circular area full of jumpy muscular yearnings; propelled by such a rich mix of motions, the club head is lucky to graze the top of the ball or get an open toe on its inside half.

The better golfer, contrariwise, seems to have only a waist, which twists slightly one way, to square his shoulders to the flight line, and then the other way, to send the club into the ball and way beyond, so that it winds up behind his back. That is what you miss on television, the quick way the center of the body, the waist and hips, slings the arms, as passive as spokes, through the swing's wide arc. The happy player gives the impression of big muscles used sparingly; the unhappy use all their little muscles, including those for pursing the lips and grinding the teeth, in order to propel a ball impossibly small and obdurate along a line as narrow and scary as a tightrope. The integrated, waisty (not wristy) swing makes the ball harder to miss; a simple coiling and uncoiling sweep it away, to distances we have trouble believing. Once I marveled at where a veteran champion had put his four-iron, way past my drive, and he bristled as if I were accusing him of cheating. As indeed, in a way, I was: it's cheating to make golf look that easy.

There is also a look the good players have of *rolling the shoulders* — for us lesser players the shoulders are a kind of seesaw, clenched and angular, whereas for our betters the suggestion is more of a tilted roundabout softly surging through a half-circle. Sam Snead exemplified this look, a kind of pantherish padded motion around his Panama-hat brim, as casually smooth as stepping onto an escalator. A fellow student of the game once came back from watching a professional tournament with the wide-eyed revelation that the pros, seen up close, aren't really swinging easy; their hands are a blur. A blur, I think, the way the end of a whip is a blur; the big body parts move the unresisting arms and loose, light hands through the hitting area before we know it. There is an enviable way in which a well-struck ball, in the moment of impact, seems already to be *halfway there.*

Good players chase after the ball with the club head. The rest of us tend to hit and quit. The difference may not be apparent, but the ball feels the difference, and quits on us in turn. Also, good players on the green express, with their springy steps and earnest squats and squints, a certain expectancy of making the putt, though it be a downhill fifty-footer. Their faith is sometimes rewarded, certainly more often than our lack of faith, with its woefully short, absentminded lags and, in compensation, nervously jabbed six-footers, which rim the cup and end up a bit more than a gimme away. Good players expect, too, to get up and down, from a sand trap and elsewhere close, where we mentally chalk up three shots — the short approach and two putts. Finally, good players are pleasant to play with as well as instructive. Snug within their low-handicap comfort zone, they maintain a cheerful temper, never condescend to a sputtering duffer, demonstrate a scrupulous but unlawyerly regard for the rules, and rarely lose a golf ball. Only when one of them hits, say, a three-wood right through the first part of a dogleg do they oblige the group to visit with them the woods, brambles, swamp, or gorse. Good golfers show what golf can and should be.

Nevertheless, they lack one lovely quality that your wristy, reverse-pivoting, heads-up, where-did-it-go buddies in the regular Wednesday foursome ever so preciously possess: you can beat them.

chapter 2

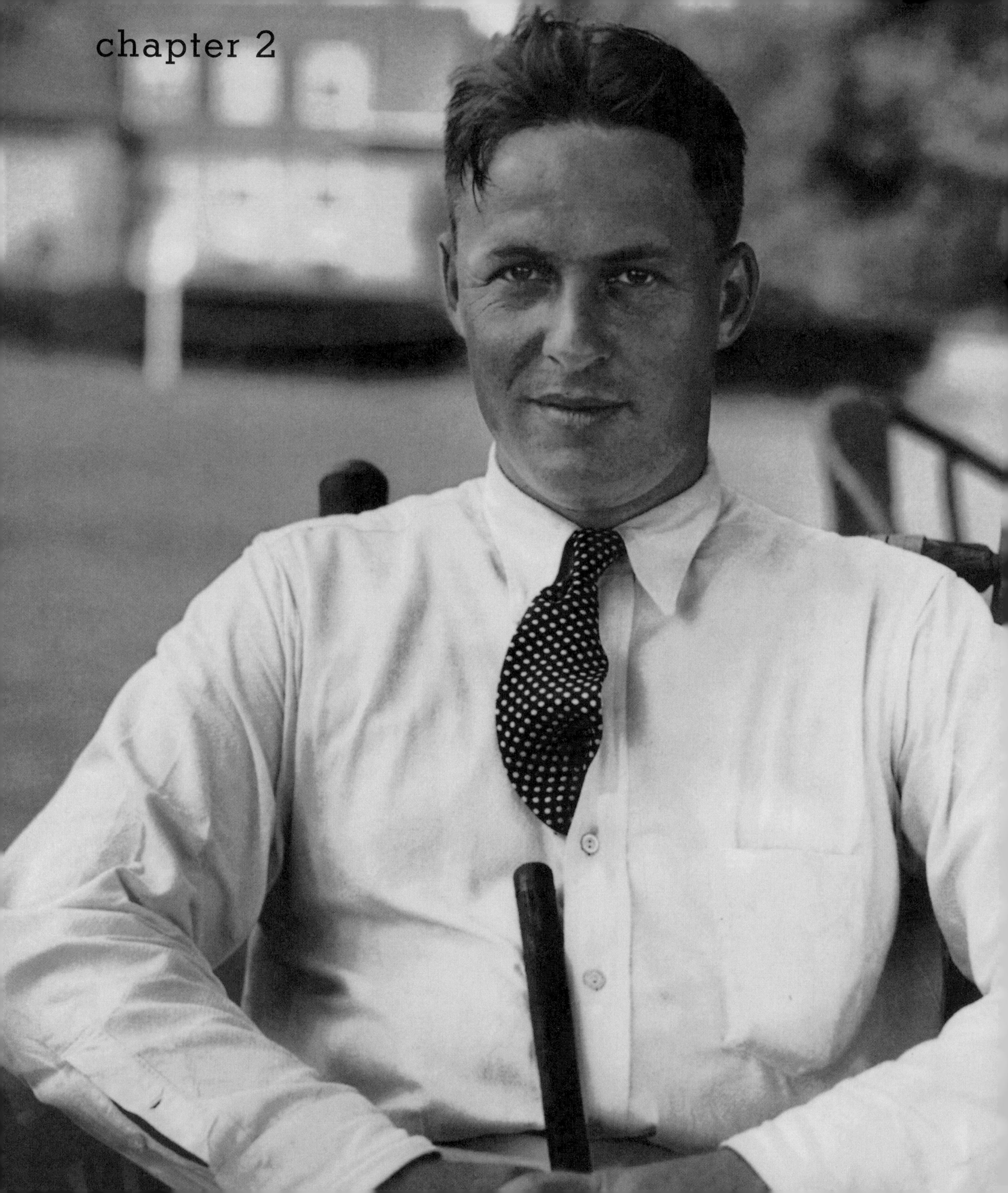

America

He was a habitual trespasser, the seven-year-old, weaving through the trees to avoid discovery. In time, he learned that his youth gave him a certain immunity, and he walked boldly across the fairways. The rich members of The Country Club didn't seem to mind his cutting across the golf course on his way to and from the Putterham School. They even let him keep the balls he found in the woods. A few years later, the boy walked *up* the fairways, as a caddie. He jumped another fence, so to speak, when he convinced school officials that he should be allowed to represent Brookline High School in the Greater Boston Interscholastic Golf Championship. This was no mean feat; Brookline had no golf team, and the fifteen-year-old hadn't started his freshman year.

BEST AND BRIGHTEST: Often called "The Bobby Jones of women's golf," Glenna Collett won her sixth and final U.S. Open against newcomer Patty Berg in 1935. Facing: Jones in repose in 1928.

Francis Ouimet was twenty and a clerk in a dry goods store when destiny picked him out of the not-yet-impressive ranks of American golfers. The occasion was the 1913 U.S. Open, held, by happenstance, at The Country Club, right across the street from the Ouimet house. The local lad had his followers—he was the reigning Massachusetts amateur champion—but the bookmakers favored Harry Vardon and Ted Ray. The British stars were on a triumphant, here's-how-it's-done exhibition tour of the States, where golf was not much older than Ouimet.

It is fair to say, then, that the firmament of golf shivered when the American youngster tied the two titans over seventy-two holes, and then shifted when he defeated them soundly in an eighteen-hole play-

off. A century later, the images linger: the elegant Vardon nervously smoking a cigarette in the rain; the mustachioed Ray lashing long drives into Brookline's deep rough; the gangly Ouimet, in plus-fours and flapping tie, striding down the fairway beside his caddie, a ten-year-old from the neighborhood. (According to legend, a Country Club member offered to carry Ouimet's bag in the playoff. Ouimet took one look at his little looper, whose eyes had begun to water, and said, "No thank you, Eddie will do just fine.") Afterward, the modest Ouimet acknowledged the ovations of his delirious supporters, collected his trophy, and walked home.

Golfers on both sides of the

Atlantic were left breathless by Ouimet's victory. The United States suddenly had a homegrown champion of international stature, a figure who, in the words of Bernard Darwin, "could work at golf like a slave and fight like a hero." What caught everyone by surprise was the suddenness of the American ascension. At the turn of the century, there had been barely enough American-born golfers to stage a good parade, and none of them could beat the best British players. But thanks in part to Vardon, who made his first exhibition tour of the States in 1900, golf had become popular at summer resorts like the Balsams in New Hampshire and the Greenbriar in West Virginia. Ouimet's victory accelerated the trend. Within a decade, the number of golfers in the United States soared from 350,000 to about 2 million, and by 1922— the year Walter Hagen became the first American-born player to win the British Open—few would deny that the game was losing its British accent.

THE APPLE TREE GANG: John Reid and a few friends established the first American course and club in Yonkers in 1888. In 1892, they built a six-hole course in an apple orchard, where, legend has it, they hung their coats on one of the trees and ate their lunch in its shade.

Golf arrived in North America before the Revolutionary War, smuggled in by Scottish soldiers and merchants. But few Americans were buying it. Golf balls were advertised for sale in New York as early as 1799, but there is no record of Filene's Basement–style battles over discounted featheries. The game itself, or something like it, may have been played in Charleston by members of the South Carolina Golf Club, or in Savannah by the mint julep crowd at the Savannah Golf Club. British sports gained little purchase in the New World—hindered, no doubt, by decades of military conflict and the burning of the White House by British troops in 1812. Baseball, not golf, caught the American fancy in the post–Civil War period, and those who preferred a less rough-and-tumble form of recreation turned to tennis, badminton, horseshoes, archery, lawn bowling, croquet, quoits, and the equestrian arts. "Golf

LADDIE BUCK: Young
loopers in the early 1900s
at the Minikahda Club in
Minneapolis, Minnesota.
For decades, there
was no better summer
job. Now, thanks to
the golf cart, caddying
is an endangered rite
of passage.

does not seem somehow to take a grip in America as does the other Scotch game," wrote an observer of the Gaslight Era. The other Scotch game was curling.

In 1887, when golf finally came to America for good, it came in the manner of a Warner Brothers cartoon—in a crate. The box, containing two dozen gutta-percha golf balls and six golf clubs, was addressed to Robert Lockhart, a New York linen merchant. Lockhart was a Scottish émigré who had played golf as a boy on the links at Musselburgh. He picked out the equipment himself on a trip to Scotland (from the inventory of Old Tom Morris's St. Andrews golf shop no less) and shipped it to New York. Back home, Lockhart tried out the clubs and balls in a park on the West Side—supposedly interrupted by a policeman, who got down off his horse to take a few swings—and then turned the lot over to his boyhood friend, John Reid, an executive at the J. L. Mott Iron Works. The following February, on Washington's birthday, Reid and five friends laid out three short golf holes on pastureland across the road from Reid's home in Yonkers, and Reid then played a friendly match with one John Upham. Reid would subsequently be known as "the father of American golf," and

Upham would forever be known as "Upham." Then, as now, there were advantages to owning the equipment.

Reid and his pals soon moved to larger pastures, including one dotted with apple trees—hence their nickname, the "Apple Tree Gang." By the end of the year, the gang had formed a club and named it St. Andrew's Golf Club—the apostrophe providing a distinguishing flourish. Within a

few years, the new club had a nine-hole course in Hastings-on-Hudson, a modest clubhouse, and a membership that included the steel magnate Andrew Carnegie.

Once sired, American golf found its legs on the Eastern Seaboard, where the moneyed class of the Gilded Age was spending much of its cash. The early 1890s saw the formation of a handful of golf clubs patterned on the imagined lifestyles of British gentry. These "country clubs" offered golf as part of a mix that included cotillions, concerts, cricket, croquet, tennis, lawn bowling, and polo. (Mrs. Stuyvesant Fish, wife of the Illinois Central Railroad president, set the tone by throwing a dinner party for her dog, who arrived wearing a $15,000 diamond collar.) With such powerful and eminent benefactors, American golf should have had

GENTLEMAN'S GAME: Englishmen Harry Vardon (left), the greatest shot maker of his time, and Ted Ray (right), the longest hitter, took time out from a U.S. exhibition tour to compete in the 1913 Open at Brookline, where they famously met Ouimet (center).

no trouble organizing itself along the lines of Britain's Royal & Ancient Golf Club of St. Andrews. It took a catalyst, however, to bring the clubs together—a sore loser from Chicago by the name of Charles Blair Macdonald.

C. B. Macdonald was a commodities broker, and the commodity in which he specialized was self-regard. Born to a well-to-do family in Canada, Macdonald fell in love with Scotland and golf while attending college at St. Andrews in the 1870s. In addition to being a businessman and a self-taught architect of pricey and challenging golf courses—he designed the Chicago Golf Club, the National Golf Links, and the Yale University Golf Club, among others—the bombastic Macdonald was arguably the best amateur golfer in the United States. That was *his* argument anyway. In the summer of 1894, Macdonald was livid when he lost a putative national championship tournament at Newport, Rhode Island, by a single stroke, to W. G. Lawrence, a Newport member. The outcome was invalid, Macdonald claimed, because he had been assessed a two-stroke penalty for hitting against a stone wall—which, in his view, was not a legitimate hazard. Furthermore, he argued, stroke play was not the established format for amateur championships.

Seeing opportunity in Macdonald's bellyaching, the St. Andrew's Golf Club promptly invited him and the other top amateurs to a match-play tournament in October, the winner to be declared the true U.S. amateur champion. Macdonald took the bait, and once again he was the runner-up, losing the final to Laurence Stoddard on the first hole of a sudden-death playoff. Afterward, Macdonald claimed that he had been ill and refused to recognize Stoddard as the national champion. A tournament was not a national championship, Macdonald said, unless it was sanctioned by all the clubs in the country.

Macdonald's argument reeked of sour grapes, but he had a point. On December 22, 1894, delegates from five of the country's most influential clubs (the Newport Golf Club, Shinnecock Hills, The Country Club, the Chicago Golf Club, and St. Andrew's) met for dinner at

CROWD PLEASER: Born in St. Andrews, Scots-American Jock Hutchinson celebrates winning the 1921 Open (in a thirty-six-hole playoff) in front of his hometown fans.

New York's Calumet Club, where they established the Amateur Golf Association of the United States, later known as the United States Golf Association, and elected the sugar tycoon Theodore Havemeyer as their first president. The new body promised "to promote the interests of the game of golf, to promulgate a code of rules for the game, [and] to hold annual meetings at which competitions shall be conducted for the amateur and open championships of the United States."

This last goal called Macdonald's bluff. When the first genuine, honest-to-goodness-we-really-mean-it U.S. Amateur Championship was held at the Newport Golf Club in October 1895, many hoped that someone in the field of thirty-six would permanently deflate the big windbag. Instead, Macdonald made short work of his first four opponents and then disposed of Charles Sands, a good tennis player but an inconsequential golfer, in the thirty-six-hole final by a score of 12–11. Through persistence, political skill, and sheer cussedness, C. B. Macdonald was the first undisputed amateur champion of the United States. On his third try.

With the pecking order of gentlemen golfers thus established, the AGAUS returned to the Newport Golf Club the following day and staged a desultory Open Championship. This first U.S. Open, a thirty-six-hole ramble in Atlantic winds reminiscent of those in Scotland, attracted only eleven players. The winner, Horace Rawlins, got a golf medal and $150—which seems generous considering that he shot 91–82. The pros, of course, were déclassé. Caddies and working men of British birth, they had come to America to manage the courses and teach the game to their wealthy patrons. "The professional, as we are now chiefly acquainted with him, is a feckless, reckless creature," wrote Horace G. Hutchinson, the first English captain of the R&A. "His sole loves are golf and whiskey." To which the professionals, no doubt, would have silently retorted: "A mon cou'd do wurse."

The truth is, the professionals did much to popularize the game in America. Vardon's exhibition tour of 1900 gave Americans a close-up look at the greatest of Britain's "Great Triumvirate" of Vardon, John Henry Taylor, and James Braid—winners, between them, of sixteen British Opens between 1894 and 1914. ("A grand player up to the green," Bernard Darwin wrote of Vardon, "and a very bad player when he got there. But then, Vardon gave himself less putting to do than any other man.") Later, Laurie Auchterlonie, the younger brother of the British Open champion Willie Auchterlonie and a member of a dynasty of St. Andrews club makers, won the U.S. Open at Garden City, New Jersey; he was the first player to break 80 in all four rounds. There was also the Scottish-born greenskeeper's son, Willie Anderson, who served as professional at several swanky clubs on the East Coast, including Apawamis and Baltusrol. Anderson won four U.S. Opens in the first decade of the 1900s, three of them in succession. Trailing Alex Smith by five strokes after thirteen playoff holes at the 1901 Open, Anderson said, "Give me a smoke and I'll win it yet"—and he did.

The foundation for American golf was already laid, then, when Francis Ouimet pulled off his stunning upset of 1913. The immediate effect was a transient burst of attention paid to golf in the sporting press. More lasting was a sudden infusion of golf into the lives of the American middle class. After the First World War, cities began to build parkland courses for the enjoyment of the public. Small towns turned cornfields into sand-green courses, making them centers of community life. "Among our golfers there was a refreshing lack of distinction as to age, wealth, social position or professional status," wrote a Wisconsin golfer of the period. "We were all brought together because we shared a love of golf." On the business front, companies like A. G. Spalding & Brothers and Thomas E. Wilson Company started to

THE HAIG: Walter Hagen played as he lived—in grand style. He delighted crowds with his knack for getting out of impossible situations. He believed, as Herbert Warren Wind wrote, that "like no other golfer, he could call upon himself for the one shot he needed and come up with it."

SHOT HEARD AROUND THE WORLD: In the 1935 Masters, Gene Sarazen had a "golden eagle" at the par 5 fifteenth in the last round. A four-wood from 240 yards cleared the lake, bounced on the green, and went in. Sarazen ended up tying Craig Wood and then beat him in the next day's playoff.

manufacture golf equipment in volume. American publishers printed golf fiction, golf biographies, and golf instructionals—the first in a trickle, and eventually a flood, of literature that has yet to subside.

From the viewpoint of the British, the growing American passion for golf must have seemed amusing—until the awareness sank in that Ouimet was just the first, and not even the best, of many provincial titans. Along came the great Walter Hagen, who walked in the front door of the clubhouse as if he were a gentleman, arrived at the first tee in a chauffeured Rolls Royce, a slinky blonde on each arm, and played hatless! And then came two-time British Open champion Gene Sarazen, née Saraceni, who was as comfortable charming strangers with his smile as he was in his workshop, grinding irons and wrapping grips. Sarazen would out-Scot the Scots by inventing the sand wedge—by conquering, in a sense, the very element from which the game had sprung. In 1922 Hagen won the British Open Championship at Sandwich, and Sarazen won both the U.S. Open and PGA Championships. Then a U.S. team captained by William Fownes defeated Great Britain and Ireland in the inaugural Walker Cup match at Southampton, New York. "To put the matter in the very plainest language," wrote *Golf Illustrated*'s Harold Hilton, "American players of the present day are better golfers than their British cousins."

The reference to cousins was apt. The Scots, in particular, embraced the interlopers as family—probably because the Americans often were. It was a literal homecoming when America's Jock Hutchinson won the 1921 British Open at St. Andrews: Hutchinson was born in St. Andrews and began his golf career there as an apprentice club maker. And then you had Edinburgh's Tommy Armour, who played for the British team in a 1921 antecedent to the Walker Cup and then turned around and represented the United States in a 1926 professional team match against Great Britain.

Sometimes, to be sure, the Scots needed time to warm up to an American star, and vice versa. When Bobby Jones, a nineteen-year-old engineering major from Georgia Tech, first saw the Old Course at St. Andrews, he thought it resembled an unimproved battlefield. Playing in his first open, in 1921, the amateur from Atlanta performed wretchedly and stormed off the course without finishing his second round. "It's a shame, but he will never make a golfer," said Alex Smith, the 1906 U.S. Open champion. "Too much temper."

Embarrassed by his behavior at St. Andrews, Jones reinvented himself. He studied English at Harvard and law at Emory University, became a paragon of sportsmanship, and learned how to overcome the final-round and final-match failures that had kept him from closing the deal in major championships. His breakthrough victory came at the 1923 U.S. Open at Inwood Country Club on Long Island, New York, where he had to overcome two final-round, out-of-bounds penalties and a disastrous double bogey on the seventy-second hole. The next day, before a crowd of ten thousand, Jones won a playoff with Bobby Cruikshank by two strokes, closing the match with a stunning 200-yard iron shot from the right rough over a guarding pond, the ball stopping eight feet from the hole. "I saw the ball on the green near the pin," Jones said afterward. "Next thing I know, somebody was propping me up by the arm."

He didn't need much support after that. Jones won most of his matches by huge margins in the 1924 and 1925 U.S. Amateurs, and in

WHIPLASH: Bobby Jones was known for his precision irons and putting touch, but his easy swing was extremely powerful. One of the longest hitters of his time, he got tremendous torque with his hickory-shafted driver.

MEDAL PLAY: In 1898, the badge of honor for the first seventy-two-hole U.S. Open went to Fred Herd, a Scotsman who spent many years as a pro in Chicago. In its first decade the U.S. Open was conducted for amateurs and the largely British wave of immigrant golf professionals.

1926 he became the first player to win both the U.S. and British Opens in the same year. In 1927 Jones successfully defended his British Open title on the Old Course at St. Andrews—which he now considered "the most fascinating golf course I have ever played"—and won the third of his record five U.S. Amateur titles. By the decade's end, Jones had thirteen victories in the four major championships of his day: the U.S. and British Opens and the U.S. and British Amateurs. "Like the man in the song, many of Mr. Jones's opponents are tired of living but feared of dying," Bernard Darwin wrote. "However, their fears are rarely unduly protracted since they usually die very soon after lunch."

Jones, a practicing lawyer at the Atlanta law firm of Butler & Yates, waited until 1930 to make his closing argument. In one storied season, he won all four major championships, the fabled Grand Slam (or, as the British preferred, "the Impregnable Quadrilateral"). He also captained a victorious U.S. Walker Cup team at England's Royal St. George's Golf Club. Already a national hero, Jones received a ticker-tape parade in New York City when he was halfway through the slam. He quickly justified the waste of paper by winning the U.S. Open in Minneapolis and the U.S. Amateur in Philadelphia. The amateur, played on the East Course of the Merion Cricket Club, rolled over for Jones; his 142 was the lowest score of the qualifying rounds, and he won his five matches by scores of 5 + 4, 5 + 4, 6 + 5, 9 + 8, and 8 + 7. In the final, a gallery estimated at eighteen thousand watched in awe as their hero politely decimated Eugene Homans, a Princeton student. When Jones closed out the match on the eleventh green, the crowd surged around him—a mob dressed in Sunday best. "Everybody admired him," Herbert Warren Wind wrote, "not just dyed-in-the-wool golfers, but people who had never struck a golf ball or had the least desire to. They admired the ingrained modesty, the humor, and the generosity of spirit that were evident in Jones' remarks and deportment."

If one heard echoes of 1913 in the praise for Jones, it was only natural. Both Ouimet and the great Bobby projected a fresh and optimistic

view in troubled times—Ouimet at the gates of hell (World War I), Jones at the doorstep of despair (the Great Depression). Their victories, as a consequence, stirred little resentment in the birthplace of golf. In 1951 the Royal & Ancient made Ouimet the club's first American captain. Years earlier, Jones got a less formal but equally heartfelt sendoff when he stopped in St. Andrews on his way to the 1936 Olympics in Berlin. Expecting to play a casual round, he found two thousand spectators waiting for him on the first hole of the Old Course. "There was a sort of holiday mood in the crowd," he remembered later. "It seemed . . . that they were just glad to see me back."

It was deeper than that, of course. The retired champion embodied the best that the game could provide, irrespective of national origin, regional accent, or political outlook. At the par-three eighth hole, where the great man drove close to the hole with a surgical four-iron shot, the crowd roared and applauded, and Jones's caddie returned the club to the bag as gently as if he were sliding a scepter into a jeweled sheath. "My," he said to Jones, "but you're a wonder, sir."

Coming from a Scotsman, it was the ultimate benediction.

SLAMMIN': Bobby Jones in 1930, hitting his approach to No. 11 at Merion, where he took the U.S. Amateur, clinching the original Grand Slam. Below: His scorecards from that tournament, where he penned "ha ha" next to a high score on one hole.

St. Andrew's Golf Club
in New York.

Winter Rules

BY WARD JUST

The day after the wretched swallows returned to Capistrano, a nor'easter tore into Martha's Vineyard with raw fifty-five-mile-an-hour winds and three inches of rain, the definitive punctuation to our three-month winter sentence of bitter cold and arctic breezes—no parole, no time off for good behavior, no golf at all. It was the worst winter anyone could recall, nuthatches belly-up in the iced-over birdbath, deer the size of racehorses foraging in the rose garden, and, cruelly enough, very little snow, so that the golf course looked playable, in the way that an inside straight looks fillable to a man ignorant of the odds. Every now and again I'd wander over to Mink Meadows Golf Club looking for a little companionship or perhaps hoping that a miraculous down-island microclimate had brought the temperature up to thirty degrees or so, only to find Lindy and the boys sitting listlessly in the clubhouse watching a French soccer match, with occasional detours to CNBC to discover just how bad the market was that day. All the gents had a golf stick in their hands. That sound in the corner was Ed bouncing a two-iron off the toe of his loafer.

This was the year 2001, a winter for television generally, especially on weekend afternoons for the Pro-Am at Pebble and the other PGA Tour events in California and Florida—the Buick, the Bob Hope, the Genuity, the Nissan, and the Honda—watching winless journeyman Joe Durant enjoy a dreamy second childhood, the one in which all putts dropped and you never met a sand trap you didn't like, and such was the sheer pleasure of it that you could honestly reply when the reporter asked the obvious question: I'm damned if I know. With his open,

honest face and cheerful manner, this Durant could be *you* long about June or July, when you'd busted 85 for the first time in your sorry life, par birdie par birdie par and so forth and if you hadn't taken a nine on the short par three you could have had a pretty good shot at 80 plain.

Lindy, this is just one of those days when everything clicked, you know?

Television winter meant also that instead of talking about your own duck hook you could talk about Tiger Woods's, along with some serious reflection about whether or not he'd lost it at age twenty-five. That young man's got to get used to the hard knocks in life, same as the rest of us. Television winter was one endless grievance. Drinking started earlier, too.

When my wife refuses to play with me, I like to play alone. I have a passion for winter golf, and not only because winter golf means winter rules. No such thing as a bad lie in January.

In winter, the Vineyard is a private, almost reclusive place, not at all summer's merry island-surrounded-entirely-by-white-wine, when you have to call a week in advance for a tee time and the parking lot is crowded with BMWs instead of pickup trucks, and there's a lot of cashmere on the golf course. After Thanksgiving, the crowds clear out, the summer houses close up, and you can show up at the clubhouse any time you want. There's a false spring in January and another in February, winter suddenly in remission, but the distant tom-toms let you know that it's only a remission, nothing to count on. Still, we've played on Christmas Day and New Year's Eve day, the sun so bright and soft you could believe it was the middle of April.

The game, too, has a different feel. I've learned some dubious tricks over the years, such as placing a half-dozen golf balls over the defroster on the car's dashboard, and then turning up the heat as far as it will go for the five-mile drive to Mink Meadows. The idea is to keep the balls in your pocket and rotate them throughout the match, because a warm ball flies farther in cold air, honest injun. Always take an extra club length on the fairway, and someone told me always to select a ball of seventy or eighty compression, though I have no idea what that means. I like the sound my metal driver makes when it strikes the ball, a sort of dumb *clunk* as opposed to the smart *click* of summer. Everything about the winter game is clunkier, the ice in the sand traps, the frozen goose turds in the fairway, the carpet of oak leaves as brittle as potato chips, the pine needles on the green. When it rains, the cups fill with water and then the temperature falls, and the flagsticks are stuck fast, often for weeks. You drive off One, a thirty-mile-an-hour wind in your face, and hope to God you can make it to the dogleg at Two and the shelter of the tall pines. At Four, the wind is at your back, and a well-struck ball will fly nearly as far as it does in August—and sometimes farther because the fairway is as hard and slippery as marble.

Hardships abound. In a heavy sweater and insulated vest, you can't swing properly. Your golf shoes slip on the clotted earth. Your nose is running and your hands are numb, so numb you can't light a cigarette. But all the same, there's a fine triumph-over-adversity spirit to the winter game. What it lacks in elegance and finesse it gains in earthiness and clumsiness, an uneven but headlong narrative. Winter golf is Dreiser to summer's Fitzgerald.

For years I have clung to the convenient theory that writers generally do not make good golfers. Writing depends on rewriting, and there's no such opportunity in golf. Play it as it lays and no mulligans, not even stately, plump ones. Agassi can easily recover from a love-game, but even Woods would be hard-pressed to come back from a nine on the short par three. When you write yourself into a hole you take the passage out of the hole and begin again. Fly the ball into the water,

you drop another ball, but you take a penalty stroke. At one time I believed that golf, specifically winter golf, was good for a writer's work. This thought was inspired by the late John Hersey, a Vineyard resident for many years and a disciplined craftsman.

John hated golf—I think for mainly political reasons. I had the feeling he believed the PGA Tour was a wholly owned subsidiary of the Republican National Committee. Nixon was a golfer. The author of *Hiroshima* was a fisherman, but not what you would call a sport fisherman. John fished for dinner. He drove his boat to that part of Vineyard Sound called Middle Ground and trolled until he had a bluefish. Then he went home and cooked it. He said that trolling on Middle Ground was useful for "back-of-the-head" work, which I took to mean thinking about writing instead of writing. Thinking about the off-key chapter eight or the always vexing page fifty-four. Thinking about the misconceived character or incoherent description. Trolling for bluefish, alone in his boat, John could ponder his work uninterrupted. The tug on the end of the line signaled dinner. A fugue state, in other words, which I thought would have application to golf, but not golf in a foursome or golf with your wife on a lovely summer's day, temperature seventy-five, no wind. In a foursome, you have to pay attention to the lie and the score, and the lovely summer's day simply offers more temptation than you could bear: front-of-the-head trumps back-of-the-head. Hersey's work was best done golfing alone in January, no one in front and no one behind, and while you're improving your lie in the fairway on Three you could be worrying also about how to improve pesky page fifty-four. Lining up the long putt on Eighteen, you could be thinking about how you're going to bring your nuvvel home—and what a surprise when the putt slides fifteen feet beyond the cup, ruining an otherwise award-winning round. And suddenly the book is forgotten in the anguish of a criminally stupid putt. I am prepared to accept F. Scott Fitzgerald's notion that a first-rate intelligence can hold two ideas in the mind at the same time. But I am equally certain that golf is not one of them.

I Prefer Merion's Towels to Augusta's, Don't You?

BY DAVID OWEN

I took up golf ten years ago, at the age of thirty-six. I was terrible, of course, but the game hooked me from the start, and I realized immediately that I wanted to play as often as I possibly could, and to keep playing for as long as I was physically able. I also realized that I wanted to write about golf. I had been a journalist for a dozen years, and I had had more than my share of interesting assignments—spending four months pretending to be a high school senior, for example, and touring London and Liverpool with a group of American Beatles fanatics, and living in a camper while traveling with a one-ring circus in New Jersey—but golf had all those other stories beat. One magazine sent me to golf school (where I cut ten strokes off my handicap), and another sent me to Ireland (where I got to stay alone overnight in the clubhouse of one of my favorite golf courses in the world), and another signed me up to participate in a three-day pro-am at a PGA Tour event (where my team came in second). In 1994, *Golf Digest* dispatched me to play the ten best courses in America and report on my experience, an assignment so wonderful that it annoyed even the editor who gave it to me.

My children, who were three and six when I took up the game, simply assumed that playing golf was what I did for a living. Gradually, I came around to their point of view. In 1995, I traveled to Los Angeles to write a story about the Riviera Country Club, where that year's PGA Championship was going to be held. I arrived in L.A. in the middle of the afternoon and checked into my hotel, which was just down the road from the club. It was too late to start working but too early to eat dinner, so I figured I would kill some time by driving over to the course and pressing my face against the fence. I had intended just to take a quick look, but a smiling guard waved me through the gate. I ran into the director of the tournament, who introduced me to the owner of the golf shop, who introduced me to the head pro, who introduced me to the club historian. Within fifteen minutes of parking

my car I was hurriedly tying my golf shoes beside the first tee, having been invited to play a few holes with a member of the board of governors and two of his friends. We made it to the twelfth before we could no longer see to putt. My new friend then insisted that I move out of my hotel and into a guestroom on the second floor of the clubhouse overlooking the eighteenth green. By the end of the week I had played golf with at least a dozen Riviera members, among them the creator of *Seinfeld,* two lawyers who had met in court while representing opposite ends of a personal injury lawsuit, and the father of Robbie Krieger, who

played keyboards for the Doors. For good measure, I also logged a few rounds at Bel-Air and Los Angeles Country Club, which, like Riviera, were designed by George C. Thomas Jr. None of my own golf made it into my story—the people I played with gradually forgot that I was a reporter, and I gradually forgot to ask them any questions—but as far as I was concerned those rounds were the point of the exercise.

In the late nineties, I spent two and a half years writing a book called *The Making of the Masters,* which was published in 1999. I did most of my research in a windowless office in Augusta National's tournament headquarters building, but on days when the weather was too nice for skimming the long-lost letters of Bobby Jones, I went outside and studied the course. (Serendipitously, my annual availability for research coincided with the club's playing season, which runs from early October until late May.) Thoroughly immersing myself in those storied golf holes was an important part of my job, I told myself, because of course the history of the Masters is written in the ground on which the tournament is contested. How could I expect to understand the genius of the twelfth hole, for example, without having pumped a few dozen of my own balls into Rae's Creek? Sadly, my estimate of how much time I would need to do a decent job—my life expectancy minus my current age—was unacceptable to everyone but myself.

I got to play plenty of golf at Augusta National. A buddy of mine at home once asked me how many rounds exactly.

"Well, I'll try to give you an idea," I said. "As we made the turn one day, we realized that we weren't going to have time to finish our round. One of the assistant pros was about to get married, and someone was throwing a party for him in the golf shop at five o'clock, and we knew that if we played all eighteen holes we'd miss the party. So we went directly from the tenth green to the fifteenth tee." (Dramatic pause.) "What I'm saying is, we skipped Amen Corner." (Another dramatic pause.) "And I didn't think anything of it." My friend collapsed to the ground with an anguished howl.

The anguish of my regular golf buddies has been one of the few drawbacks of my new career as a golfer (other than the occasionally irate incomprehension of my wife, who doesn't play). Some of my assignments have simply been hard for my friends to bear. As a result, I've become somewhat slower to volunteer my opinion about (let's say) the fickleness of the wind on the seventh at Pebble Beach, or the quality of the caddies at Dar es Salaam, or the various interesting differences between the showers at Merion and the showers at Pine Valley. I don't want to make life miserable for

my friends, because the truth of the matter is that despite all the golf I've played on glamorous courses all over the world, most of the rounds that stand out most prominently in my memory are ones I've played with my regular buddies on my own little nine-hole course at home. The lesson is the same one my mother taught me when I was twelve and had just returned from six weeks at summer camp in Colorado with a dozen rolls of grainy black-and-white photographs of what had looked, at the time, like breathtaking terrain. Twenty years from now, she said, you won't care about these mountains; next year, take pictures of your friends.

Not that I regret any of my trophy rounds. In fact, some of them still give me the chills. There was, for example, the round I played at Augusta National on the Sunday before the 1998 Masters. It was the last day before the course would be closed to noncompetitors, and I was playing with two members of the club and the producer of the CBS tournament telecast. We had set up a match between the green jackets and the media, and the green jackets were winning. As we stood on the sixteenth tee, the producer and I were deep underwater and running out of presses. But I birdied the sixteenth (eight-iron, six-foot putt). Then I birdied the seventeenth (driver, lob wedge, fifteen-foot putt). Then I eagled the eighteenth (three-wood, pitching wedge). Four under par on the last three holes—and I have the plaque to prove it. The first two guys to congratulate me, outside of the members of my foursome and our caddies, were Ernie Els and Lee Janzen, who had been playing a practice round just ahead of us.

Other than stuff like that, though, I pretty much keep these things to myself.

The putting green at
Bethpage State Park Golf
Club on Long Island,
New York.

chapter 3

Equipment

He started with two Popsicle sticks glued to two sugar cubes, and it was your job to guess what it was. A television remote control? A stapler? An electronic calculator? (This was a man, after all, who had worked on the ground guidance system for the Atlas missile.) It wasn't until Karsten Solheim inserted a stainless-steel shaft between the sugar cubes that you got the picture: it was a putter—or as Solheim would describe it when he filed for a patent in 1959, "a golf club head having one or two face plates or platens connected at the toe and heel through two blocks to a torsion bar having a hosel connected to it for receiving a shaft." The heel-toe balance, he explained to anyone who

WOODWORK: The MacGregor Chieftain (with ivory back weight) from the late 1920s was the top-of-the-line MacGregor wood. Facing: In a GE laboratory in 1932, scientists measure the speed of the 1930 National Driving Champion Jim Reynolds's drive as it connects with a golf ball. It measured 125 miles per hour.

RUBBER-CORE ERA: A collection of rubber-core balls and a practice ball. Left to right, top row: Silver King SW1, MacGregor baseball-pattern practice ball with cork center, and Double Dimple ball. Center row: Farroid, Lynx, Super Harlequin, and Wonderball. Bottom row: U.S. Tiger, The Star Challenger, and Washington White.

would listen, made the blade more resistant to twisting on off-center hits, while the torsion bar got the ball rolling with desired over-spin.

There was just one problem. When Solheim putted balls with a steel prototype, the club head did not produce a comforting *click* as it contacted the ball. It went *ping*. Solheim didn't know whether the touring professionals, who were unadventurous about equipment, would go for a putter that sounded like a sonar echo. (The pros would have problems enough with the putter's appearance, which resembled a bad piece of plumbing.) He went ahead anyway. In the winter of 1960, Solheim drove to Monterey, California, the trunk of his car crammed with putters to show the pros on the putting green at the Bing Crosby National Pro-Am. Each putter had "PING" stamped on the sole—because sometimes you can hide a liability by treating it as a selling point.

It turned out well for Solheim. The man with the Colonel Sanders goatee sold millions of putters over the next forty years and lived to see his homely invention used to win more than eighteen hundred professional tournaments. As founder and CEO of Karsten Manufacturing

Corporation, Solheim also reinvented the golf iron. In 1961 he introduced the concept of perimeter weighting, which increased the so-called sweet spot by distributing more weight to the edges of the club head. He was also the first to apply the "lost wax" or investment-casting process to the manufacture of irons, a breakthrough that made consistency possible throughout a set and breathed life into small foundries around the world. He even invented the lob wedge—probably after gluing a potato chip to a straw.

As unique as he was, Karsten Solheim knew he was just one in a line of tradesmen and inventors who, over the centuries, have sought technological solutions to golf's intractable problems. "We'll never be able to develop a ball or a club that will let you shoot 18," says Bill Morgan, the golf ball development chief for Titleist. "But from the very beginning, the player with the best equipment had an advantage. If you had a good rock, it went farther."

Consider, for a moment, the rock. In the game's prehistory, when players used tree limbs or shepherd's crooks to advance the ball, the critical property was roundness. An acorn flew farther than a bird's nest; a round rock rolled better than a flat one. The ancient Romans, who were masters of contrivance, made their own *sphaerae* by stuffing feathers or hair into a leather case and painting the panels. Later—probably about the time golf clubs began to resemble hockey sticks—someone tried making golf balls out of wood. (This was not a reach. Wooden balls were used in *jeu de mal* and pall mall, and the first polo balls were carved from the roots of willow trees.) In these early ball wars,

RABBIT, RUN: In 1934, a woman operates the rabbit golf ball machine, which increased internal pressure in the golf ball by as much as eight pounds per square inch to add ten yards of distance.

THE TROON CLUBS: At the end of the nineteenth century these two irons and six woods were found inside a boarded-up cupboard along with a Yorkshire newspaper dated 1741. Experts believe the clubs may date to the early 1600s.

the clear winner was the Roman-style ball, which provided the "softer feel" that ball marketers love to this day. Unfortunately, to make such a ball a St. Andrews pro like Allan Robertson needed several hours to stuff a hatful of feathers into a leather casing, using an awl that pressed uncomfortably against his chest. (Sewing up the little buggers was no picnic, either.) Featheries were so expensive and so fragile that hardly anyone could afford to play.

That's why the invention of the gutta-percha ball, in 1848, ranks as the most important development in the history of golf. It took little effort and almost no skill to hammer strips of coagulated tree resin into a mold; a child could learn how to do it in a day. In no time, ball production soared and unit price plummeted, making the game affordable for ordinary gentlemen and stimulating the design of new courses. When the ball makers discovered that the new orbs flew straighter and hung in the air longer after they had been scuffed up, they began to etch aerodynamic grooves into the covers—decades before the Wright brothers took off from Kitty Hawk and flew about as far as a modern tee shot. By the end of the nineteenth century, the British firm of A. G. Spalding & Brothers was manufacturing gutties on two continents and marketing the gold-standard "Vardon Flyer"—a pebble-surfaced ball that the English champion Harry Vardon promoted on his 1900 American exhibition tour.

The guttie gave way, in turn, to the rubber-cored ball, patented in 1898 by the Americans Coburn Haskell and Bertram Work. The Haskell ball had an interior of rubber bands wrapped under tension around a hollow rubber core and held together by a balata cover. Not surprisingly, this lively package took off like a rocket and soared like a glider. Detractors called it "Bounding Billy" and warned that course hazards would be made obsolete, but the new technology insinuated itself into the game. In 1901 Walter Travis successfully defended his U.S. Amateur title using a rubber-core ball. A year later, Sandy Herd won the British Open with a Haskell—a feat made more salient by the fact that every-one else in the field played a guttie. "It was perhaps a pity that the [rubber-core] ball was ever invented," wrote Bernard Darwin in 1946, "but there never could be any question of going back."

A century later, the wound ball was still the professional's ball of choice—almost every winner on the PGA Tour in 1999 played a ball containing tightly wound rubber bands—but most middle and high handicappers had switched to so-called two-piece balls with solid rubber cores and durable Surlyn covers. These solid-core balls flew much far-ther, but the best players preferred a soft-covered ball with a high spin rate, a ball they could stick close to the hole with backspin "juice." That was the case, anyway, until Tiger Woods switched to a solid-core ball in the spring of 2000. When Woods won three major championships that summer, including the U.S. Open by fifteen strokes and the British Open by eight, the major manufacturers of golf balls threw dust covers over their ball-winding machines and boosted production of solid-core

PEG IT: In 1899, George C. Grant patented the first wooden tee. For hundreds of years, golfers had used sand to form a mound on which to place the ball, but Grant—one of the first African American den-tists—disliked dirtying his hands before every hole.

IRON AGE: In the late 1800s, once the idea of subdividing the cleek and lofter irons was accepted, a wide variety of iron clubs sprang forth, including the Mashie, the Niblick, and the Jigger. The first iron (left) is from the mid- to late 1700s. The next two, with oversize blades, are from the late 1700s or early 1800s. The concave and hooked face of the fourth iron dates it to roughly 1850. The fifth— a Carrick lofter (a driving iron)—goes back to 1880. Finally, Spaulding's "Rob't. T Jones" five-iron dates from 1931.

balls with urethane coatings. Ironically, when Woods was putting well, he would say, "I'm really rolling my rock."

The history of club making shows more divergence and eccentricity than that of ball making, clubs not being limited to a single size or shape. The first dedicated golf clubs were probably fashioned by shipwrights and bow makers—the former because their work with masts and spars made them experts on flexible joints, the latter because they understood the elastic properties of wood.

Typically, the eighteenth-century club maker used a bow saw to cut a banana-shaped head out of a block of blackthorn. He then joined the head to an ashwood shaft in a long, shallow-angled splice called a "scare," which was secured by a whipping of fisherman's twine coated with pitch. The grip was made of sheepskin or calfskin and was much thicker than in modern clubs; old-time golfers held the club in their palms, as if tugging on a rope. After 1820 the preferred shaft material was Tennessee hickory, but not hilltop hickory (too brittle) or swamp hickory (no spring). "The best hickory," writes the golf historian David Stirk, "came from halfway up the hill." If truth be told, the best players would have climbed a mountain for the right shaft. "It is infinitely easier to get a head to suit you exactly," said the five-time British Open champion James Braid, "than it is to get a perfect shaft."

With their files, chisels, and glue pots, the early club makers produced a variety of long-nosed, shallow-faced clubs: "play clubs" for hitting off the tee; lofted spoons for ground strokes; and baffing spoons for hitting a kind of drop-kick pitch shot. The only iron clubs carried before the popularization of the gutta-percha ball were the small-headed "rut iron," which fit like a dentist's probe into narrow wheel ruts, and the comblike "track iron," which was used to advance a ball lying among stones. But as soon as the feathery was extinct, the club makers began to lose business to the blacksmiths and metalworkers, who hammered out various iron-headed clubs: cleeks for tee shots, mashies for fairway shots, and niblicks for pitch shots. These craftsmen called themselves "cleek-makers," and for about a century they maintained a nervous coexistence with the club makers. In the end, of course, they all wound up under the same factory roofs as employees of big sporting goods companies like Spalding, Macgregor, and Wilson. And then they dwindled almost to nothing, as the investment-cast process turned golf club manufacturing into a connect-the-components business.

Nevertheless, the game continues to be equipocentric, its gear nudged to higher and higher performance levels by men wearing faraway looks and pocket pencil protectors. In 1926 the USGA authorized the use of steel-shafted clubs in its competitions; the R&A followed in 1929, and suddenly golfers no longer had to worry about the altitude of hickory trees. A few years later, the great Gene Sarazen pondered a more specific problem—the unreasonable difficulty of chipping balls out of sand bunkers—and solved it by soldering lead onto the back of a niblick to create a wide flange. His invention, the sand-iron, helped Sarazen win the 1932

PUTT FOR SHOW: With its intricate engravings, the early-1800s McEwan putter is one of the most beautiful and prized early clubs.

Utility clubs circa 1900.

British Open with a record score of 285, and it became, next to the putter, the most essential club in the modern player's bag. "I was trying to make myself a club that would drive the ball *up* as I drove the club head *down*," Sarazen explained—sounding a little like the fellow who defined a putter as "a club designed to hit the ball partway to the hole."

Among the more recent club-making breakthroughs that have met with universal acceptance are matched sets of clubs with graduated lofts (by George Nicoll, 1926); perimeter weighting of club heads (by Solheim, 1960s); the investment-cast process (by Solheim again, 1960s); the development of the metal wood (by Gary Adams, the founder of Taylor Made, 1970s); and the perfection of oversize drivers (by Callaway Golf's Richard Helmstetter, 1990s). "There is no other game where an

industry as sophisticated as that which put men on the moon has been created to put grooves on golf clubs [and] broom handles on putters," writes Michael Parkinson of the *Daily Telegraph*.

All this innovation has pleased consumers and made cash registers ring, but one occasionally hears a principled dissent. In the 1980s, the American champion and course designer Jack Nicklaus challenged ball manufacturers to do the unthinkable: design a ball that would *not* go farther. At about the same time, the PGA Tour, the USGA, and the R&A touched off a legal war by banning the PING Eye2 iron, Karsten Solheim's latest invention, on the grounds that its square grooves reduced the skill level required to impart backspin. The square-groove imbroglio was eventually settled at great expense to the PGA Tour, but the relationship between the equipment companies and golf's ruling bodies became more adversarial as nasty arguments arose over the "spring-like effect" of driver club faces and the allowable "coefficient of restitution" of a golf ball. "Golf is supposed to be fun," cackled Ely Callaway, the founder and CEO of Callaway Golf. "We're just makin' the game a little easier for the average player." Former USGA President Sandy Tatum countered, "When the manufacturers talk about innovations, they're talking about reducing the skill factor of the game. They're not talking about the sport but the bottom line."

At the heart of the argument is the fear that the technology genie, if allowed to get more than an arm and his head out of the lamp, will push the game to the point where it is unsustainable. Yes, a par five of 1,000 yards might be appealing to golfers in the year 2100; but every yard added to a golf course requires a commensurate increase in greens fees to pay for its upkeep. Yes, it would really be something to watch a sixty-year-old Tiger Woods fly his tee shot on the first hole of the Old Course over the Swilcan Burn and make it suck back to the hole for a tap-in eagle, but it won't be so thrilling if you can do it, too.

The debate has been going on for as long as golf has been played. Bernard Darwin, writing in 1946, remembered the years following World War I as a rabbit-ball era. ("The long hitter became so long that there remained for him hardly such a thing as a good two-shot hole.") Steel shafts were okay by the USGA in the 1920s, but grounds for disqualification by the R&A. When Walter Travis used a center-shafted, mallet-headed "Schenectady" putter to win the 1904 British Amateur, the R&A immediately instituted a prohibition on center-shafted putters that lasted more than thirty years.

The rules of golf, in fact, twitch every time some Gyro Gearloose comes out of his basement workshop with a smile on his face and a club

WARHEAD: Named after a World War I cannon, the Big Bertha exploded onto the golf market in the 1980s and is still the dominant driver today. Golfers believe that its oversize head makes the ball go farther.

in his hand. Rule 4.1 requires that "all parts of the club shall be fixed so that the club is one unit" (no pivot-hung pendulum putters) and "shall not be designed to be adjustable except for weight" (adios, Dial-a-Club). The shaft "shall be generally straight" (no slinkies?). The club head "shall have only one face designed for striking the ball" (anticipating the Six-Faces-of-Eve multi-lofted metal wood), and the club face "shall not have any degree of concavity" (rendering it useless as a garden spade). Appendices 2 and 3 of the rules go even further, stipulating that the axis of a putter shaft "from the top to a point not more than 5 inches (127 mm) above the sole must diverge from the vertical in the toe-heel plane by at least 10 degrees when the club is in its normal address position," while warning that a golf ball will not conform to the rules of golf "if the mean of the difference in carry is greater than 3.0 yards, and that value is significant at the 5% level, *or* if the mean of the differences in time of flight is greater than 0.20 seconds, and that value is significant at the 5% level."

One could fairly accuse the rules makers of being extraordinarily anal, if they didn't have ample evidence that golfers will try anything. At its headquarters in Far Hills, New Jersey, the USGA maintains a collection of dodgy equipment submitted by overreaching inventors: putters that stand up by themselves, chipping clubs with attached arm braces, club heads with trailing skis, wedges with pebbled inserts to impart extra spin, golf balls that fly forever, and golf balls that don't curve.

It's not easy to separate the silly from the sublime, to distinguish the genius with Popsicle sticks and sugar cubes from the crackpot with Velcro and sleigh bells. In 1994 a Russian trade delegation approached American aerospace foundries with a weird proposal: to sell them surplus titanium recovered by cutting up scrapped nuclear submarines. It was the Americans' job to imagine a commercial use. Masts for racing yachts? Ski poles? High-priced cutlery? "There are many applications for a material so strong and so light," said the Russians. A year later, their melted submarine hulls reappeared in the form of $500 titanium drivers, the must-have golf clubs of the 1990s.

These clubs, too, produced a distinctive sound: *Ka-ching.*

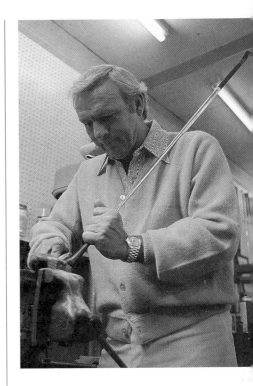

METAL HEADS: Left, the patent drawings for the original PING perimeter-weighted irons. Above: Arnie grinding away in his workshop. Palmer got the club-tinkering habit from his greens-keeper father.

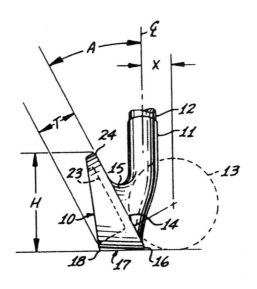

Patented April 11, 1972 3,655,188

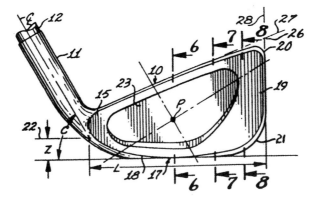

INVENTOR. *KARSTEN SOLHEIM* BY *Lindenberg & Freilich* ATTORNEY

The Joys of Risk

BY
JOHN PAUL NEWPORT

The first time I realized I was a good golfer, or might actually become one, was on the par-five eighth hole at Montauk Downs, a couple of years after I started playing golf again as an adult. My drive had landed in the rough on the side of a steep hill, three inches below where my feet would be when I tried to hit it, and some 230 yards from the green. In front of the green was a wide, swift-running stream.

Rather than lay up short of the water as any "smart" player would, I squatted awkwardly, whaled away with my three-wood, and watched in delight as the ball cleared the stream and spun to a stop five feet from the cup.

My playing companion that day was a morose TV comedy writer. He looked at me standing on the side of the hill, then up ahead at my ball on the green, and then back at me. "You're a good golfer, John Paul," he said.

Two things stand out vividly about this moment. First, my friend couldn't have cared less about my ability. He was just making an observation. Over the years I have come to accept this as normal among golfers. Remember all those dreadful shanks you hit, which you were sure set off gales of inward snickering among the others in your foursome? They didn't even notice. Golfers are way too preoccupied with their own fragile games to pay much attention to anyone else's.

The second thing that stands out about the moment is the thrill beyond reason of having pulled off the shot. Primarily, I think, the thrill was caused by the water hazard in front of the green. Without that stream threatening to gobble up my ball, I could have hit a mediocre shot without much consequence. I could have dribbled the ball down onto the grassy flats anywhere short of the green and still have made par with a short pitch and a couple of putts. But the stream focused my concentration, set my heart to thumping double-time, and coaxed a shot out of me that I hadn't known I was capable of hitting. The hazard transformed the hole into something edgy and intense.

In the dozen or so years since that day, my handicap has improved into the low single-digit range and I can report that playing at this level is filled with unanticipated pleasures. One is the quiet satisfaction of having made progress on a long-term project. My knowledge of the game and its subtle secrets continues to grow with each passing season. Another more visceral pleasure is hitting a higher percentage of my shots *pure*. Far from getting used to the almost erotic rush of this experience—the magic of somehow generating explosive power out of nothing but ease and rhythm—I find that pure shots are more thrilling than ever. The cumulative ecstasy of hitting, say, ten pure shots in a single round is far more powerful than the merely additive pleasure of hitting an equal number of such shots spread over a month.

And all these pleasures are turbocharged by the presence of risk. Producing a pure, powerful drive on the practice range is wonderful. Blasting that same drive down a narrow, tree-lined fairway in the late stages of a match with something significant on the line—that's sublime. Risk makes everything about the game sweeter.

I can't claim to have read extensively in the field of evolutionary psychology, but I tend to believe that we humans are hard-wired to thrive on risk. Nowadays we sit behind desks and are loaded up with insurance—we don't get to confront much risk anymore. Golf (for me, at least) helps fill the gap. Granted, the risks in golf are trumped up, but the sweaty palms and rapid pulse rates they inspire are real. And the better you get, the more claim those risks lay on your soul.

When I reacquainted myself with golf as an adult, my expectations for any given shot were quite modest. I was always delighted to hit a beauty, of course, like that three-wood at Montauk Downs, but I knew I was just as likely to hit a screaming slice. Basically, nothing surprised me. I got upset at bad shots, naturally, but my frustrations were a blunt instrument and quickly morphed into little more than simple-minded self-loathing. Now my disappointments are more nuanced. My skills have reached the point where my expectations are precise and the emotionally acceptable margins for error are much narrower than they used to be. A screaming slice is intolerable—and yet it still sometimes happens. A seven-iron that hits the green but doesn't stay below the hole is an agonizing failure. A seven-iron that does stay below the hole but got there via the wrong trajectory is a source of anxiety, as perhaps indicating an insidious new swing flaw. I am acutely aware of many more specific risks with each shot than I ever was before, but the upside is that when I am on my game, when I am performing at the outermost edge of my ability, I am also aware of transcending all those risks, and the resulting high is exhilarating, almost surreal.

That emotional punch leads, inevitably, to a craving for the even more intense risks of formal competition. "There is golf and tournament golf," Bobby Jones famously said, "and they are not at all the same thing." Tournament pressure is basically the anxiety of risk amplified and extended over time—for the full duration of a round, or of several rounds, as opposed to just for a select few shots per round. Dealing with tournament pressure is a skill in itself. The hardest part for me is overcoming my fears enough to swing the lazy, easy rhythm that produces my best shots. Tournaments infuse every stroke with an extra, sparkling dose of danger, which is narcotic for the connoisseur of risk. Now all this may seem like a prescription for ruining a perfectly good game, and in one sense that's what happens when you get better. These days when I play golf after a long absence and my swing is not in tune, or when I find myself playing in corporate outings or other purely social situations, the game can seem a little bloodless. I sometimes feel as if I'm trying to recreate some bygone thrill.

The loss of golf as it used to be is acceptable, however, because in exchange I have substituted a richer, adult pleasure—one that, ironically, I think of as closer in spirit to the unfettered play of childhood. I come to this conclusion from observing my six-year-old daughter, Anna. Some of the time when she plays, she laughs and skips and frolics, as children in our imagination always do. But at least as much of the time—when she is building a fort, say, or working a puzzle, or mastering hopscotch—she furrows her brow, concentrates hard, and wholly gives herself over to the task at hand, much as I do when I am playing golf. The common denominator is that we both believe. When Anna plays with dolls she isn't pretending to inhabit her dollhouse universe; she actually believes that she is. The same goes for me inside the risk-enhanced kingdom of golf.

But the connection to childhood goes even deeper. I am often tempted to tell Anna not to be in such a hurry to grow up. Like most kids, she is irrepressibly eager to get to the next stage in life: to quit using a car seat, to get her ears pierced, to have as much homework as the big kids do. But I stop myself because I realize that one of the things that make being six so wonderful is the urgency of the desire to be seven. Take away that innocent faith in the inherent superiority of being one year older and *whoosh*—you might as well be my age, forty-six. Needless to say, I have no especially urgent desire to turn forty-seven. But I do have a mostly unexamined faith that being a six handicap instead of a seven, or a scratch instead of a two, *is* something worth getting excited about, and I'm grateful for this compulsion, provided I can keep it under control. It's one of the only direct links I have left to the passion of my youth.

I would like to point out, however, that none of the above applies to the misery of putting. Putting is an annoyance and a riddle that can never be solved.

Starkisms

BY CHARLES MCGRATH

My first golf teacher, when I was about twelve, was a leathery old pro with whiskey breath. From him I learned an overlapping grip, which I still have, and that I wasn't good at taking lessons. I decided to seek further instruction from the place where, at that point in my life, I had learned everything else of importance — books — and I spent hours reading and rereading Ben Hogan's *Five Lessons: The Modern Fundamentals of Golf.* This is a classic and justly revered text, but as anyone knows who has tried to put its principles into practice, it is marred by a signal flaw: the swing it describes doesn't really work — isn't remotely achievable — unless you happen to be Hogan, and certainly not if you happen to be a gangly, bookish twelve-year-old. After a couple of years of fruitless and solitary study, I gave golf up. I announced at the time that my defection was on political grounds — golf was too Republican — but had I been more honest I would have admitted that frustration had something to do with it as well. Hogan's imaginary glass plane had become a yoke around my neck.

When my apostasy finally ended, some thirty years later, I came back to golf through the same door I had left by — reading about it. In my ardor, though, I overapplied myself, and like someone who has studied so many sex manuals that he is hopeless in the sack, I soon found myself in need of a therapist. For a few months I consulted weekly, in an upstairs room in Manhattan, with a certified swing doctor who analyzed my woeful condition with a videocamera and a computer that tracked my weight shift, swing path, and

club-head speed. He made a few adjustments in my stance and posture, and when they didn't work told me to forget them. I terminated therapy no better than I had been before, but arguably no worse, and possibly I was even wiser. I knew enough, for example, to seek emergency first aid when, next season, I developed a case of the screaming shanks while on a golf trip down south. The young assistant pro I saw not only straightened out the shank but showed me how to hit down on the ball and compress it, so that for a moment I was hitting my seven-iron 170 yards. I can't do it anymore, of course, but I have the videotape he gave me, and there I am — or rather, a virtual, otherworldly me — launching lovely parabolic rockets.

And then — here a little skirl of bagpipe music would not be inappropriate — I met John Stark, and my approach to the game was changed forever. He turns up in my dreams sometimes, lashing his big, powerful swing into the wind, and when I'm on the course I often hear him talking in my ear. "Och, aye — a golf shot!" he'll say, or more often, when I've chunked one, "No, no, that's not it at all!"

Stark, who retired a few years ago as the head pro at Crieff Golf Club, is to Scotland roughly what Harvey Penick was to Texas — a revered, slightly eccentric teacher who instilled in generations of golfers not only the fundamentals of golf but a deep appreciation of the game and its traditions. He's a big white-haired man with a ready laugh and a Glasgow accent that makes him sound a lot like Sean Connery. As a teenager he had a promising amateur career; in 1953, when he was just

eighteen, he tied Ben Hogan (for second) after the first round of the British Open at Carnoustie. He thought briefly about playing on the pro circuit, but, he says, "My heart was never really in it. I liked to laugh too much, and I didn't have the stomach. Besides, my real talent was for match play, and match play was going out the window." Instead, he became a club professional, first in Scotland and then for nine years in Sweden, where the game was just getting started and where Stark was, in effect, one of the pioneers. He came home, to Crieff, in 1962, and by then he was a learned and outspoken philosopher of golf, with both an advanced understanding of swing mechanics (he can imitate, on the spot, the swing of any pro you name) and a profound distrust of golf theory. What he really believes in is touch and feel, and occasional moments of magic.

Three years ago, after reading about him in Michael Bamberger's book *To the Linksland,* I spent the better part of a week with Stark. The photographer Macduff Everton and I traveled with him from Crieff, in the central highlands, all the way down to the Mull of Kintyre. We looked at courses, with an eye to what made them uniquely Scottish; we played a few rounds; and we talked golf for hours—or rather John did, spellbindingly, and he also dipped liberally into the inexhaustible store of caddie anecdotes that has made him a much sought-after after-dinner speaker. Many of his stories involve Pipey Matheson, the legendary caddy at Royal Dornoch, who is famous for his impatience with low tippers and slow players. God help you if you're both. Stark claims to have been there, for example, on the day when someone who had taken two hours to play the first nine asked Pipey the yardage to the tenth. Pipey shook his head and replied, "I dinna think we'll make it before dark."

I thought I had been playing pretty well—for me, at least. (I parred the windswept final four holes at Machrihanish, for example; the others we won't talk about.) But two days before I was to leave John said to me, "Let me show you a thing or two about your swing," and for the next forty-eight hours he deconstructed my entire golf game.

It has been said that Stark teaches no two people the same way. In my case the approach was tough

love. He started with my chin (not high enough) and worked down through my shoulders (too active) and hips (spinning out), to my feet and knees (too rigid). The only thing he liked was my waggle. Unfortunately, time (and my own waywardness as a pupil) did not permit Stark to reassemble all the pieces, and ever since I have been trying to finish the job on my own. Even now, years later, the meaning of something he said will reveal itself to me in a new way, and for an instant the light will go on: so *that's* what he meant. "Keep the shape," for example. This basic Stark mantra, I realized just recently, refers to what others mean when they talk about maintaining the proper spine angle, but it also envisions the ideal shape of the swing itself and the importance of staying long through the ball. It's as if my hours with him were a time-release pill, still dissolving years later in my golf brain.

I kept a notebook of Starkisms, and I refer to it often, as much for their tone and attitude as for specific advice. Here are some of my favorites:

• If you have a consistent flaw, *polish* it. If you have an inconsistent flaw, get rid of it.

• When you practice your long game, give yourself a good lie. When you practice your short game, work from a patch as bare as a badger's arse.

• There's no one way to swing. Remember, the ball doesn't know how the club head got there.

• What's all this business about yardage books? If you're a twenty handicapper, they're useful only if you're lost and want to know how far it is to the clubhouse.

I also have a tape I made by putting a little recorder on the ground next to the practice tee while John was giving me a lesson. Every now and then I listen to it and pick up another little morsel of wisdom I had forgotten about. "On the downswing, keep your head back against the shot," for example. But mostly what I hear is a *splatting* or a *thwapping* sound (me, hitting fat), followed by John's voice: "No, stop." "No, no—that's bad!" "Try it again." "A little better." "Oh, Christ—no!" "Do it again." Periodically this woeful litany is interrupted by another, different sound— a *swish* followed by a magical little *click!* That's Stark, demonstrating the right way, and in my mind's eye I can still follow his shot, climbing steadily upward into the Scottish sky, with just the sweetest little hint of a draw.

Listening to golf like this brings back a flood of memories—of Stark's piercing blue eyes and jack-o'-lantern smile (he wears his uppers only for photographs and special occasions); the way, late in the Creiff afternoon, the rooks rise in a cloud and migrate, cawing, from treetop to rooftop. But listening is also a fundamental Stark principle. He actually encourages his pupils to practice with their eyes closed. "You want to feel the big muscles in your back," he says, "and you want to concentrate on rhythm and balance. You want to listen to the sound of your own swing. Hear that *swicht?* Aye, that's a golf shot. If you do this, just swing with your eyes closed. Believe me, it will do you a world of good."

And it will. It may not improve your score, or not right away. But it will get your head out of books and put you in touch with another, better teacher—the one inside you, the silent pro, who is just dying to be consulted, if only you would pay attention for a change.

Sometimes they just don't work. A frustrated Tommy Bolt rejects his driver at the 1960 U.S. Open.

chapter 4

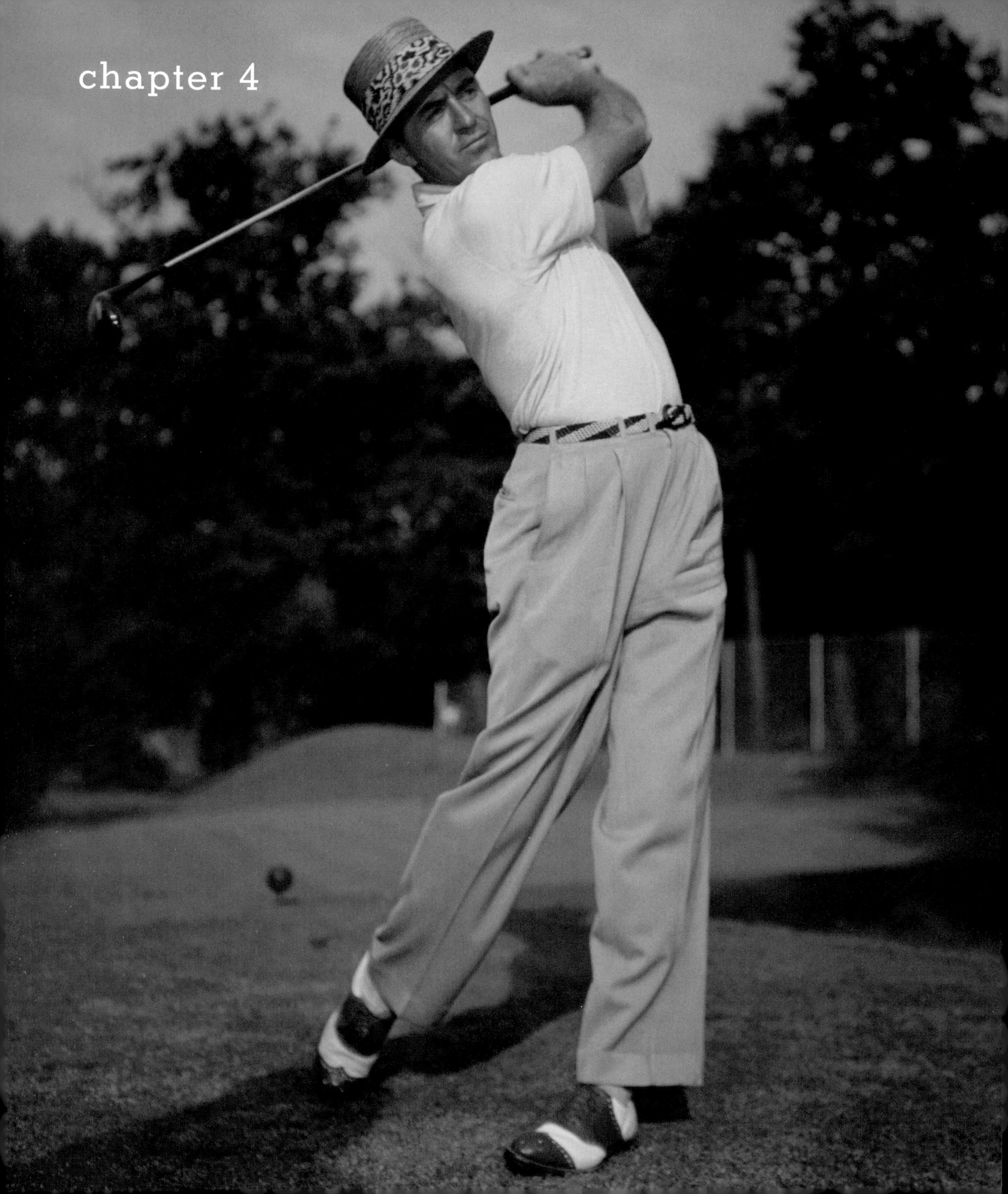

The Early Tour Years

Contrary to popular belief, the PGA Tour did not begin in the late 1950s, when Arnold Palmer began hitching up his pants on television, or in 1969, when George Forrester began paying players $50 a week to wear caps bearing the name Amana. No, the stream of prize money began in 1895, when Willie Park Jr. played Willie Dunn on three Long Island courses for $600. It burbled along without form or name until 1916, when the Professional Golfers Association was formed. Sometimes the tournament players shared a channel with an honest promoter like Fred Corcoran, who booked Sam

KINGS OF SWING: Natural-born golfer Sam Snead (facing) never took a lesson in his life; Ben Hogan (above) put in endless hours with the game's most exacting tutor: himself.

TAKE DEAD AIM: Jack Redmond, trick shot artist, tees off from New York's Whitehall building in 1930. In the tour's early years, pros typically made more money from exhibitions than they did from prizes.

Snead into Chicago's Wrigley Field so he could hit a two-iron from home plate over the scoreboard in center field. Other times, the pros went down the lazy river with gamblers and grifters like Titanic Thompson, who preferred their decks stacked and their pigeons fat.

At the turn of the twentieth century, of course, there was hardly any such thing as a tour. There was barely a circuit—just a hodgepodge of "opens" at which club professionals could shake off the rust and compete for small purses. Most of the tournaments were played in the South in the winter, golf having become the rage in resort towns at the turn of the century. The first professional event with any shelf life was the North and South Open at Pinehurst, North Carolina, won in 1902 by Alex Ross (brother of Donald) and in later years by the likes of Byron Nelson, Ben Hogan, and Sam Snead. The PGA's own showcase, the PGA Championship, was not launched until 1916, when the New York chain-store owner Rodman Wanamaker donated a silver cup for a trophy in exchange for rights to sell discounted golf equipment in his stores. That first PGA Championship, played at Siwanoy Country Club in Mt. Vernon, New York, was won by James "Long Jim" Barnes, who beat Jock Hutchinson in the final, one-up. Barnes later authored the first photographic golf instruction book.

Prize money in those days didn't support a bachelor pro, much less a man and his family. The typical club professional on the eastern seaboard made his living selling golf equipment and giving lessons. If he was lucky, he found winter employment at one of the Sun Belt resorts, and if he was good with a niblick, he supplemented his income by playing money matches with wealthy tourists and other pros. Golfers of real stature, like Barnes and Hutchinson, made their money by cracking jokes and performing trick shots at one-day exhibitions. Walter Hagen, who played close to two thousand exhibitions in his lifetime, was Will Rogers without the lasso.

By the 1920s, as Sun Belt chambers of commerce learned how to milk national publicity by staging pro tournaments, the opens began to rival the exhibitions. The most lucrative tournaments were the Texas Open, which got started in 1923 with a strong field and $5,000 in prize money, and the Los Angeles Open, which debuted in 1926 with the biggest purse in golf history, $10,000. It would be

a stretch, however, to compare these nascent events to the organized spectacles of the modern PGA Tour. "There was a circuit," writes Al Barkow in his history *Golf's Golden Grind*. "But its wiring was something an electrician might hook up after losing his manual."

To become a tour in the modern sense, the winter golf circuit needed what circuses had—an advance man, someone to negotiate tournament dates, line up sponsors, make travel arrangements, and garner publicity. The first of these golf tour impresarios was a sportswriter named Hal Sharkey, who quit after a year of spadework. The second was Walter Hagen's personal manager, the memorable Bob Harlow.

In August 1929, Harlow became the PGA's first full-time tournament manager. He was college-educated, a gourmand, and a man of considerable organizational and promotional skills. Harlow released starting times a day in advance so that newspapers could publish them. He printed the tournament standings with the leaders listed on top. Harlow also introduced player entry fees, fines and suspensions, courtesy transportation, exemptions from qualifying for the best players, and most important— because it is the cornerstone of the modern PGA Tour—the use of volunteers as tournament help.

Harlow's successor, a blarney bag named Fred Corcoran, ran the tour from 1937 to 1948. Corcoran was, in the words of golf writer

Charles Price, "a man whose office was in his hat and who never thought any idea was ridiculous as long as it was original." His most colorful stunt was the "Music Match" of 1940, in which Gene Sarazen and Jimmy Demaret played an exhibition match with prizefighters Jack Dempsey and Gene Tunney, while Fred Waring and his Pennsylvanians followed on a rolling stage, drums thumping and saxophones squawking. Corcoran proved that promotion paid. In a single decade, he took the PGA Tour from a regional circuit of twenty-two tournaments to a year-round tour of forty-five tournaments. "He took the game away from the Scottish peasants," Bob Harlow joked, "and gave it to the American peasants."

PACKING THEM IN: Honey-tongued Boston promoter Fred Corcoran (left) was the first to put the professional tour on solid financial footing, and no pro benefited more than Byron Nelson (right).

Harlow and Corcoran didn't do it all by themselves, of course. Their road show was blessed with some gifted performers, men of substance and personality who knew how to please crowds. The most marketable of them was Samuel Jackson "Slamming Sammy" Snead, a Virginia hillbilly with a swing as smooth as syrup and a repertoire of blue jokes as deep as a vaudevillian's. Snead won the third PGA event he played in, the 1937 Oakland Open, with four rounds in the 60s, and when Corcoran showed him his photo in the *New York Times*, the young man famously asked, "How'd they ever get my picture? I ain't never been to New York." Before long, Snead's picture was everywhere, almost always with a fedora or a coconut-straw hat covering his receding hairline. Between 1937 and 1965, Snead won a

Bobby Jones on the tee at the 1948 Masters with (from left to right) Bobby Locker, Dick Chapman, and Ben Hogan.

PGA-record eighty-four tournaments, including three Masters, three PGA Championships, and the 1946 British Open.

Just below Snead on the star chart was the occasional band singer from Texas, Jimmy Demaret, who won the Masters three times between 1940 and 1950. Demaret was a blithe spirit with a ballroom dancer's taste in clothing and a comedian's gift of repartee. (Grousing about air turbulence on a flight to Japan, he cracked, "Lindbergh got eight days of confetti for less than this.") If you didn't like Demaret, you could always follow his temperamental opposite, the tall and gloomy Ralph Guldahl. Guldahl won back-to-back U.S. Opens, a Masters, and a PGA Championship in the late thirties, but lost his form while writing a golf instruction book and ultimately dropped off the tour.

For an even starker contrast of temperaments, fans of the early tour looked to two rivals from Texas, Byron Nelson and Ben Hogan. The loquacious Nelson and the taciturn Hogan met as boys, when they caddied at Fort Worth's Glen Garden Country Club. From the beginning, they were competing paradigms. To Nelson, the world seemed a place of opportunity—he was like Francis Ouimet in this regard—and the people in it a source of support and empowerment. To Hogan, the world was hostile, a black forest of treachery and pitfalls; he fixed a

skeptical eye on most anyone who crossed his path. He and Nelson were friends, to the extent that Hogan would allow, but it was not a warm relationship. "I was never in Ben's home," Nelson recalled years later, "and I didn't have his private telephone number."

Because of his unconflicted nature, success came more easily to Nelson. His first win in a major championship, the 1937 Masters,

was followed by a fortuitous triumph at the '39 Open, which owed as much to Sam Snead's collapse at the seventy-second hole as it did to Nelson's final-round 68. But Nelson was clearly one of the game's best players, winning PGA Championships in 1940 and 1945 and beating Hogan in a playoff at the 1943 Masters. In 1945, in a pre-retirement flourish that still confounds students of the game, Nelson won eighteen tournaments, eleven of them in a row. It's true that the fields in that final year of World War II were slightly depleted, but Snead played most of the season, and Hogan returned from an Army stint to play in the autumn, his game sharper than when he left. Nelson's 1946 scoring average of 68.33 still stands as a PGA Tour record, and witnesses to his feats invariably put him on a pedestal. "Nelson frequently seems to use no wooden tee like mere mortals," wrote Dan Jenkins, a promising sportswriter from Fort Worth. "Tosses the ball on the ground, moves it around for a second with the clubhead of a 1-iron or a 3-wood—and whap. Splits the fairway. Walks briskly to the ball. Couple of waggles with the iron. Splinters the flagstick."

Hogan, by way of comparison, played the tour for nine years before breaking through, winning the 1938 Hershey Fourball with Vic Ghezzi. Then, having tamed his demons and his chronic hook, he led the tour in official earnings from 1940 to 1942, only to have his momentum broken by two and a half years in the Army Air Corps. No sooner had Hogan returned, in fact, than Nelson *retired,* at age thirty-four. In the thirteen postwar months when they competed together, both Texans played extraordinarily well. Hogan shot a tour-record 261 at the 1945 Portland Open, and Nelson answered, two weeks later, with a 259 at the Seattle Open. Hogan won ten tour events in the stretch, and Nelson, playing in fewer tournaments, won five. Hogan led the 1946 money list; Nelson won the Vardon Trophy for low stroke average. Figuratively speaking, the putter was passed in Oregon at the 1946 PGA Championship at the Portland Country Club. Nelson, worn out and anxious to start his new life as a rancher, lost by a hole to Porky Oliver in the quarterfinals. Hogan then beat Oliver in the thirty-six-hole final, 6–4, for his first major title.

With his nemesis gone, Hogan imposed his dour presence on the game so thoroughly that grim began to look good. A man who practiced obsessively, he would hit balls, it was said, until his hands bled. Hogan's accuracy inspired such awe that his peers often stood behind him on the practice range to study his swing, to watch his ball flight, and

sometimes just to listen. ("The sound of club against ball and turf was strangely different," Barkow wrote.) Golfers began to talk of a Hogan "mystique" and speculate over his "secret"—whatever trick of hand or torso that enabled him to hit shot after shot with robotic accuracy. Hogan, however, revealed little. When a young pro asked him for advice, the great man asked, "Do you have any practice balls?"

THE ICEMAN COMETH: On his first trip to Scotland Hogan won the 1953 British Open. Back in New York, he was the first golfer since Bobby Jones to be rewarded with a ticker tape parade.

When the young man nodded eagerly, Hogan said, "Then use 'em."

In the seven years following Nelson's retirement, Hogan won eight major championships. Six of those wins came after he crashed his car into the front of a bus in West Texas and spent two months in a hospital, his body reduced to ninety-five pounds of mending bone and occluded veins. His near-fatal injuries notwithstanding, Hogan rejoined the tour in 1950 and won the U.S. Open at the hilly Merion Golf Club in a Sunday playoff with George Fazio and Lloyd Mangrum. Three years later, Hogan swept three of the four modern majors, winning the Masters, the U.S. Open at Oakmont, and the British Open at Carnoustie (in his only try for the claret jug). In those days, the PGA Championship was played the same week as the British Open, making a true Grand Slam impossible, but the returning Hogan was given a New York ticker-tape parade as joyous as the one for Bobby Jones in 1930. "I've got a tough skin, but this kind of brings tears to my eyes," Hogan told a crowd at City Hall. "I don't think anything can surpass what's happening now."

Despite these occasional flashes of portentousness, tour life was still a road show. The players traveled to most tournaments by car, chipping in for gas money and amusing each other with stories as mile after mile of bumpy macadam *throp-thropp*ed under the wheels. One time Herman

Keiser and Bob Hamilton were driving behind a car filled with several pros, including the irascible Ky Laffoon. Keiser spotted sparks under the car, and thinking that maybe their tailpipe was dragging, he sped up and waved his friends to the shoulder. When the lead car stopped, Laffoon leaned out the window and held up a club he'd been dragging. "I'm just grindin' down a wedge," he said.

The road was both dull and dangerous. Sam Snead remembered driving a Model A Ford from Hot Springs, Arkansas, to Miami in 1935. "Going down through Georgia, there were one-way wooden bridges that might be 300, 400 yards long, and you had to look ahead to see if there was anyone at the other end coming on. Cows would be sleeping in the middle of the road, and you'd have to be careful at night, because they were black and black-and-tan and blended with the road." At journey's end, the players would check into a guest house or a rustic motel. "It was nice on a cold Texas night," Charles Price remembered, "to sit on the cracking leather chairs among the potted palms and the jardinieres in the lobby and listen to *Amos 'n' Andy* or Bocke Carter, the Walter Cronkite of radio, on the Philco behind the front desk." If the players were big shots, they might glide up the drive to a resort hotel, where flags flapped and doormen wore coats with epaulets the size of notebooks. Frank Stranahan, the talented amateur and muscle man, liked to watch bellhops struggle up the steps with his suitcases, which were filled with free weights.

It was a milieu of hustlers and welchers, soft touches and leeches. Leonard Dodson, winner of the 1941 Oakland Open, would bet on anything—which crow would be the first to fly off a telephone wire, which raindrop would be the first to slide to the bottom of a window. Chandler Harper, who won the 1950 PGA Championship and seven other PGA events, once played a notorious no-pay for two-dollar skins in a rainstorm. "Making him pay after each hole, I ended up with a pocket full of one-dollar bills that were wet as hell," Harper said later.

MUSCLE MAN: Frank Stranahan, Champion Spark Plug heir, was the first golfer to believe in weight training; he liked to carry dumbbells in his suitcase— much to the surprise of hotel bellboys.

Lurking at the periphery of tour life were the out-and-out scammers and professional gamblers. Titanic Thompson, while not quite good enough to play on tour, was equally proficient right- or left-handed. In a typical sting, Thompson would win a money match with a stranger playing right-handed, and then double the bet while agreeing to play a subsequent match left-handed, with strokes. Other times, Thompson offered to step aside and let his pint-sized caddie finish the match for him—his caddie being the notorious Doc Yockey, a scratch player himself.

The betting fraternity was not limited to the Damon Runyon types, who flashed pinkie rings and wore white ties with black shirts. Bobby Jones and his New York stockbroker friend Clifford Roberts enjoyed a gentlemanly wager. The club they founded in the 1930s, the Augusta National Golf Club, was a nest of upper-crust self-indulgence, a place where powerful men could drink, bet, and play golf in a secure and beautiful setting. The club's steward, Bowman Milligan, staged prizefights in a ballroom at the Bon Air Vanderbilt Hotel, and the closing bout was usually a "battle royal" in which a half-dozen black youngsters with boxing gloves were put into the ring. ("Everyone would start swinging," Roberts wrote in his biography, "with the last boy on his feet being declared the winner.") During Masters week, the action centered on a public Calcutta auction at the Bon Air and a members-only pool at the club, but professional bookmakers had free run of the grounds. Until 1949, when the USGA and PGA cracked down on gambling to protect the game's image, spectators, sportswriters, and the players themselves placed their Masters bets at the course. Keiser, a twenty-to-one shot in 1946, complained afterward that certain club members, who had bet up to $50,000 each on Ben Hogan, had tried to sabotage his play by changing his Saturday starting time and sending him out for the final round with a thirteen-year-old caddie. Keiser fondly remembered two bookmakers — "the fat guy from New York and the little guy from Texas" — who lent him money on

the weekend so he could bet on himself. Keiser got $2,500 for winning the Masters and about $1,000 more from his wagers.

Over time, Jones and Roberts deemphasized the Masters-week hijinks, but the stakes for the golfers became higher, and the rewards greater than mere cash. Horton Smith got $1,500 and a gold medal for winning the inaugural in 1934, when the tournament was called the Augusta National Invitational. Gene Sarazen got something more with his victory in 1935 — a crystal bowl and a niche in golf history for his final-round four-wood shot to the fifteenth green, which went in the hole for a double eagle ("the shot heard round the world"). Within a decade, the Masters was counted as the fourth, and in no way the least, of the professional majors. To the novelist John Updike, the Masters was "green grass, green grandstands, green concession stalls, green paper cups, green folding chairs and visors for sale, green-and-white ropes, green-topped Georgia pines. If justice were poetic, Hubert Green would win it every year."

The green that mattered to the pros, of course, was the kind with pictures of presidents on it. From 1934 to 1942, total annual prize money at the Masters never budged from its initial level of $5,000, and

TEST DRIVES: Bobby Jones tries out a new hole at Augusta as it's being built. The course was designed to emphasize strategy above all, and virtually every tournament has been decided by challenge and disaster on the back nine on Sunday.

Facing (bottom): Some of the first professional women stars embark on a trip to England in 1951. From bottom: Betty Bush, Betsy Rawls, Peggy Kirk, Betty Jameson, Patty Berg, and Babe Didrikson Zaharias.

Ben Hogan putts on the eighteenth hole in the 1955 U.S. Open at the Olympic Club in San Francisco. He was upset in the next day's playoff by Jack Fleck.

VALE OF TEARS: The scenic 485-yard tenth hole at Augusta National, which slopes left and drops one hundred feet from tee to green, is the site of two famous playoff disasters: Ballesteros's crash and burn in 1987 and Scott Hoch's two-foot miss in 1989.

checks were rarely issued to players who finished lower than twelfth. The tour as a whole didn't see big purses until the 1950s, when successful businessmen like George May of Chicago, Robert Hudson of Portland, and Waco Turner of Ardmore, Oklahoma, began staging big-money tournaments. In 1954, after Snead beat Hogan in a Masters playoff, May announced that he would pay an extra $25,000 on top of an already gargantuan $50,000 first prize to Snead or Hogan if either won his All-American Open. Hogan, underwhelmed, didn't even bother to enter.

Most pros, however, continued to act like bloodhounds at the first sniff of money. Doug Sanders, speaking for several generations of players, said, "I'm working as hard as I can to get my life and my cash to run out at the same time. If I can just die after lunch Tuesday, everything will be fine." Even young Arnold Palmer, driving from tournament to tournament in his coral pink Ford, tapped the steering wheel to the rhythm of the car radio and flipped his cigarette butts out the window, never dreaming that he would one day be richer than the men who staged the tournaments.

Single File

BY MICHAEL DILEO

A few years ago, my regular foursome broke up like a bad marriage. Dave, the magazine editor with the low fade, moved from Austin to New York; Robb, cookbook author and master of the five-wood recovery shot, took a new job in Houston; and Alan, the long-hitting Sicilian restaurateur, had a baby, opened a new Italian place, and gave up the game.

Following Elisabeth Kübler-Ross's paradigm, I went through the stages of grief rather rapidly: denial, blame, despair, bargaining, buying a new putter. After all, I'd gotten used to playing with these guys, the gambling and gossiping, the communal schadenfreude over gagged five-footers. Suddenly I was forced to deal with Supreme Court–level questions concerning the true nature of the game: Is golf social or existential? "Solitary golf is barren fun . . . ," Updike wrote, "as pointless as a one-man philosophical symposium." There was only one thing to do: I was going to have to take muny-course potluck and become a walk-on.

I tried to convince myself that my loss was a good thing. After all, there was a great big world out there of new people to play with. Furthermore, this was my chance to work on my game. The very comfort of our regular group could have been holding me back. Prom date–level butterflies plagued me the first time I went stag to my home eighteen, Lions Municipal, an old, tree-lined, inner-city course simply called "Muny" around here, nestled in between the O. Henry Middle School and Town Lake, with a great recumbent stone lion guarding the practice green. The squawk of the loudspeaker announcing a seven-minute call for "Mike-single"—I used the short version of my first name for maximum regular-guy effect—unnerved me. How should I act? What was default mode for a single? Would they assume I was a hacker or fear me as an unknown ace? Which one was I anyway? What were my clothes—Banana Republic golf shirt, sneaker-like white Nike Air golf shoes—and my clubs, old PING Eye2 berylliums, a Hawkeye driver—saying about me?

A threesome awaited on the first tee, two plumbers who knew each other, and a fellow walk-on, an airline pilot named Rick. I don't recall much about my round; all my self-absorption dissolved in my fascination with my partners of the moment, particularly Rick.

He was forty-something with bleached-blond hair and weight-room biceps, trying a bit too hard, and a Doug-Sanders-in-a-phone-booth tachycardiac swing that lived in searing contrast to his placid exterior. Clearly, this was a guy with some issues. A split personality seemed to be at work. Golfer Rick was a borderline hysteric, as evidenced by the spastic flinch he made at the ball, but the in-control pilot persona would reassert itself nanoseconds after impact. Midround he developed a terrible case of the shanks. After each scalding right-turn rocket into the woods, he'd utter only one soothing epithet: "Interesting . . . ," the syllables drawn out languidly. It must be a pilot thing, I assumed. Copilot: "Sir, number-two engine's on fire." Captain Rick: "Interesting . . ."

In the weeks that followed, I, Mike-single, kept a journal of my walk-on rounds, intending to fill it with techniques, tips, and swing thoughts. Instead, my pen kept turning to the people I met, the astounding biodiversity of golf swings and exposed neuroses out there in the great Galápagos Islands of municipal golf. There was Marty, for example, moon-faced and pear-shaped, wearing a red cardigan, looking like Bobby Knight's gentle little brother, who took the club back in a quick handsy manner until the shaft struck him hard in the back of his head, the crack of True Temper on cranium positively audible, a swing so profoundly masochistic it gave *me* a headache. He broke 90, somehow, without breaking his skull. It was his way of triggering the downswing, Marty explained when I got up my courage late-round to ask about his swing, a guard against hitting from the top, and while there was mild discomfort, he'd become used to—no, virtually addicted to—the pain. In a way, Marty stood for all golfers, the masochistic self-torturer in each of us.

And there was Tom, with the raptor eyes, short

haircut, and sweet swing of a club pro, who cursed a savage string after even the most minor mis-hit, and who, when we reached the thirteenth tee, confessed without flinching that he was a Lutheran minister. And Dave, who walked the course with his miniature Pinscher named Mama, trained to sit still as a Kalahari bushman while her master putted. And the unnamed heavy drinker with a cooler full of beer on his pull cart, knocking one back on each of the first nine holes, until he went into the men's room at the turn and never returned. And the old farts, three guys who'd been crew members together in World War II, who took me to the cleaner's playing dollar skins.

The litany of American jobs I encountered reads like a miniature Dos Passos novel: Bob the wool broker; Jaime the pediatrician; Jerry the meteorologist. And, this being a musician's town, all the band people: Mario, who claimed to be married to the singer Shawn Colvin, and who certainly did indeed take many cell phone calls from a clearly demanding spouse; Carl, the roadie for heavy metal bands, who claimed to have played golf, high on life, with Willie Nelson; John, who plays cello for Lyle Lovett; and Richard, the sound man at a local nightclub, who wore a hooded sweatshirt that made him look like the evil emperor in *Star Wars* and who knocked down a whole box of Altoids in one round.

My favorite section of the golf journal, a virtual

verbal shrine, is devoted to the women, those rare jewels, all the more precious for their scarcity, who dared to intrude on the patriarchal realm of the municipal course. Jordan, for example, was an athletic-looking Arizona blonde who'd played on her high school team. She talked mostly about her hatred of then-President Clinton, all her arguments dittoed from old Limbaugh broadcasts, but, hey, nobody's perfect. Had I been her Svengali, a fantasy I admit to indulging, I would have cut down on her forward press, a move so unsubtle it overly delofted her irons, leading to some seriously bladed screamers, but aside from that Jordan could play.

Karen, on the other hand, was a dabbler in golf, not finishing most of the holes, playing only to share the company of her apparent paramour, a simian, cigar-chomping financial planner with the perfect name of Cash. Dark-haired and lightly freckled, she was dressed all in crisp whites, a vision from a better time, her voice so soft and cute she sounded like a child. On the third hole, a bee landed in her cup of beer and she freaked, begging me, as Cash was off in the trees with his mashie at the time, to extricate it, which I did without incident. I would have swallowed it live if she'd asked me to. When I inquired about her panicky reaction, she answered in the most endearing whisper, "I've never been bitten or stung by anything."

For unforgettable presence, though, and felicitous effect on my play, no one compares to Marianna. I didn't notice her at first, that sultry summer day, as I approached the tee. A man was there, darkly Latin, soap-opera handsome, taking long fluid swings with his driver. His name was Francisco, and he said he was from Mexico City and he was taking courses in international law at the local university before joining an American firm later in the year.

I talked him out of the driver; 205, 210 maybe, is all you want on the short dogleg-right first at Lions. He creased a long iron with a gentle fade. I was impressed.

Then his wife emerged from the shadows, a dark beauty wearing a white men's shirt, tails tied in front, baring her midriff. While her husband studied, she said, she was working as a cook at a nearby hotel. "I live for

food," she said, her accent a lush mouthful. "To cook it, eat it, dream about it."

Of course, Marianna couldn't play a lick. Her indifferent three-quarter swing could only advance the ball in fifty-yard worm-burners. She giggled passionately at her own misses, though, so I loved her anyway.

I cannot say for sure that it was because of Marianna, but I played lights-out that day. I'd been improving slowly since the foursome died, thinking my way around the course better, but this day I was absolutely in the zone. I made the turn one-over.

This would have been brilliant, except that it was two strokes worse than Francisco. He had a lot of game, simply overpowering the wily, double dogleg, par-five eighth hole with a monstrous drive, a soaring six-iron over a copse of live oaks to six feet, and a dead-center eagle putt. Still, I hung close, grinding out pars, getting up and down. Only very rarely have the competitive fires emerged in my walk-on days, but I began to want to beat Francisco that day.

As we strolled the steamy fairways in a hallucinatory cloud of summer heat, I regaled Marianna with my best tales of traveling in Mexico and encouraged her to keep playing, despite her string of cold-topped Surlyn-slashers. When she began to mention some of her husband's annoying habits, his overfocus on golf, his lack of spontaneity, I felt a guilty thrill.

Late in the round, I made a string of putts and drew within a stroke of Francisco, who seemed at last aware of our unspoken rivalry, even chunking a little pitch on the fifteenth. When I missed the seventeenth green and he knocked a seven-iron stiff, though, he had me. Still, a par on the last hole gave me a year's-best score, and even better, a farewell hug from Marianna. As I walked off basking in her glow, a thought nagged at me. What if I had played so well, not because of her, but because of him?

Some new golf buddies have turned up of late, and the formation of another regular game beckons. Even so, I could never give up the identity of Mike-single completely. It's too wide and weird a world out there in the vast unmapped territory of the walk-on.

Hogan Lore
escapes again

BY DAN JENKINS

It's not giving anything away to say that Ben Hogan was no lounge act in Vegas. The Wee Bantam Ice-mon Hawk coming out to do twenty minutes of one-liners, warming up the crowd for Louie and Keely.

Nope. Wasn't him.

But I'll tell you what else he wasn't—and I can say this because I knew Ben better than any other sportswriter, living, dead, or somewhere in between. He wasn't the nation's most feared badman, some kind of John Dillinger the Feds chased across golf courses for twenty years but failed to ambush because his wife Valerie wouldn't wear a red dress.

Coldhearted guy. That was the cliché perception many people had of Hogan. People who only knew him from a distance and saw a hawk-eyed fellow drawing on a cigarette, deep in thought, measuring another golf hole for demolition. Or people who only knew him from a single moment in his presence and may on that occasion have found him silent, abrupt, even rude.

Ben didn't suffer fools, it's true. Idiotic questions didn't amuse him. And if you approached him and he didn't already know you, he probably didn't care to know you and might insinuate it with a look. And he could steer himself into such depths of concentration while competing in a U.S. Open, Masters, or PGA Championship that he often didn't recognize a close friend in the gallery. Or didn't appear to.

Here's what Ben was, if you were lucky enough to know him reasonably well, and perhaps more important, if you knew the game of golf: a painfully shy man, a loyal friend, a man with a surprisingly dry sense of humor, a

person who admired hard work in an individual—and had no respect for anything less—someone who answered intelligent questions thoughtfully, the most incredibly observant individual you'd ever meet, a perfectionist in as many things off the golf course as he was on, such as his impeccable manner of dress, the care with which he made golf clubs, and the painstaking efforts he made to see that his food was prepared properly.

I can only talk about the Ben Hogan I knew. A man who was one of the most cooperative athletes I ever logged time with in my entire career as a journalist-typist, a man who wrote thank-you notes to me when he liked something I'd written about him in newspapers and magazines, a man who invited me to play countless rounds of golf with him in his heyday, and finally a man who requested in his failing days of 1997 that I be among the pallbearers at his funeral.

In other words, I did not know Ben Hogan the tyrant. Ben and I became friends, and I began enjoying a working relationship with him in the spring of 1950. That was the year he was fighting his way back to full stride from the head-on crash between a Greyhound bus and his Cadillac that almost killed him in early February of '49.

Our common ground was Colonial Country Club. Colonial was Ben's home course at the time. It was mine as well, thanks to the generosity of an extraordinary gentleman named Marvin Leonard, the club's founder, who'd invited the TCU golf team to call it home back then.

There were golf writers in other cities in the fif-

ties, of course, but they didn't have Ben Hogan. Most of them had Joe Zilch. I realized even then how fortunate I was, and I'm grateful to this day for the access I had to Ben when he was at his peak.

Curiously, this meant there were times when I'd find myself being interviewed by other writers, like at the Masters, somewhere on the road.

"What did Hogan do last night?" a guy would ask urgently.

I'd provide my standard answer, as if I actually knew: "He bathed his legs in hot water for an hour, ordered a club sandwich from room service, and played gin rummy with Valerie."

"Did he say anything?" I'd be asked just as urgently.

My reply: "Yeah, he said 'Gin' a lot."

Around Fort Worth, three or four times a week I'd leave the paper or the campus and drive the five or ten minutes over to Colonial, go straight to the pro shop, and ask, "Where is he?"

I'd hear from somebody that he was over on Eleven, or down by Fifteen, or out by the sixth. Off practicing somewhere on the course.

I'd grab a cart, go find him, sit and watch. He'd nod, acknowledge my presence, then keep hitting balls to a shag boy, who never had to move very far to pick them up.

One day in the spring of '51 I watched him hitting something weird and couldn't resist saying, "What the hell is that?"

He was hitting choke-grip, knock-down three-irons about 165 yards.

"I need it at Oakland Hills," he said.

I don't recall that he used the shot at Oakland Hills when he captured one of his five U.S. Opens, but he had it in his repertoire.

These were the days, all through the fifties, when he might finish hitting practice balls and say, "Let's go." Meaning, let's go play nine or eighteen. Sometimes it would be just the two of us, sometimes he'd ask a member or two to join up. I must have played thirty or forty rounds with him throughout the decade.

He was aware that I could play golf without in-

juring myself or anyone around me. He'd been known to ride around in a cart with Marvin Leonard and watch a few holes when we'd play a college match at Colonial—four singles and two best-balls, gallant TCU Horned Frogs against Texas Longhorns, Rice Owls, Texas Aggies, SMU Mustangs, and other dreaded opponents.

There's pressure for you. Play a college match in front of Ben Hogan.

If there were four of us in the recreational games at Colonial, the balls would be thrown up to decide partners, and we'd play a one-dollar Nassau, no limit on your basic presses.

A person didn't always win if he had Ben for a partner. I vividly recall the afternoon a member and I holed every putt we looked at and soundly thrashed Ben and his partner. Afterward Hogan paid off to me personally. I should have framed the one-dollar bill he handed me, but I spent it on a date.

By now you must be eager to know what I learned, or to put it better, what I remember best, from all those years of hanging around the guy. Well, for one thing, I learned to overclub. That's because Ben over-clubbed. It may have been his real secret, aside from practice. He overclubbed 90 percent of the time, and not simply because he was always striving for distance. He firmly believed that it gave him more control over the shot.

Especially downwind. "You always overclub downwind," he said. The reason was, you wanted to "bounce it in," and by overclubbing you'd be trying to "take something off," and if you came up short, that was okay.

He insisted there was more trouble over a green, by and large, than in front. Being long almost invariably presented you with a tougher chip shot, tougher bunker shot, or tougher slash out of the rough.

"But you can't overclub if you don't play golf all the time, and don't practice," he said.

Ben played by "feel" and often said, "I don't want to know the exact yardage to the green—I may want to hit a three-iron."

I learned what the favorite clubs in his bag were. The brassie, five-iron, seven-iron, pitching wedge. He could turn a brassie into a driver or into a four-wood, whichever one he might need at the moment. If called for, he could turn a five-iron into a seven-iron, and a seven-iron into a nine-iron, and I never saw him hit a pitching wedge from more than ninety yards away.

I learned what his favorite courses were. One was Colonial, as you might guess, but back in the fifties when it was a tighter, trickier, tougher par-70 golf course. Others were Seminole in Palm Beach, Riviera in Los Angeles, Brook Hollow in Dallas, Southern Hills in Tulsa, Pinehurst No. 2 in the sandhills of North Carolina, and Augusta National.

He always said that if he could play only one course the rest of his life it would be Seminole. His favorite stop on the tour, back before the accident when he played a full schedule, was the elegant old North and South Open in Pinehurst. Great course, charming surroundings, black tie for dinner, but maybe he was fond of it because he won the North and South three times.

I learned that apart from Byron Nelson, who

came from the old hometown, Ben's best friends on the tour in the early days were Henry Picard and Ky Laffoon. And in later years his best pals were the entertaining, outgoing guys whose personalities he envied—Jimmy Demaret, Sam Snead, Tommy Bolt, Claude Harmon, Jackie Burke Jr.

That Hogan and Snead, who were such rivals on the golf course in the forties and fifties—and in the immortality derby—were actually good friends somehow managed to be a well-kept secret from the fans and from most of the press.

Looking back on it all, I've decided that the best thing I ever learned from Hogan came during that exhibition round at Colonial to which he had condemned me. I'd tried to get out of it, but he commanded me to complete the foursome with himself, his brother Royal Hogan, a former city champion, and Raymond Gafford, a fine local pro.

It was a beautiful spring day in '56, and I should have made it a point to get out there in time to hit a few practice balls before I shot my usual 77, but I didn't. Something at the paper detained me. So I arrived on the first tee just in time to tee off—and just in time to notice about five thousand spectators lining the first fairway, a 565-yard par-five.

All I hoped was that I wouldn't kill somebody with a duck hook when I swung the driver, but the Old Skipper allowed me to hit a decent drive down the fairway. He was sparing me for something more humiliating.

Which was the following: I topped my second shot with the three-wood. Went about twenty feet. Almost fanned it. Then I topped it again, maybe fifty yards. Then I topped a five-iron. It scooted about thirty yards.

It was while I was trudging toward my ball to try to hit my fifth shot, either hearing laughter from the crowd or imagining I could hear it, and wishing I could crawl into a hole and disappear, that I realized I had company walking beside me. It was Ben Hogan, who said with a glint: "You can probably swing faster if you really try."

To this day, it's the best golf tip I've ever had.

chapter 5

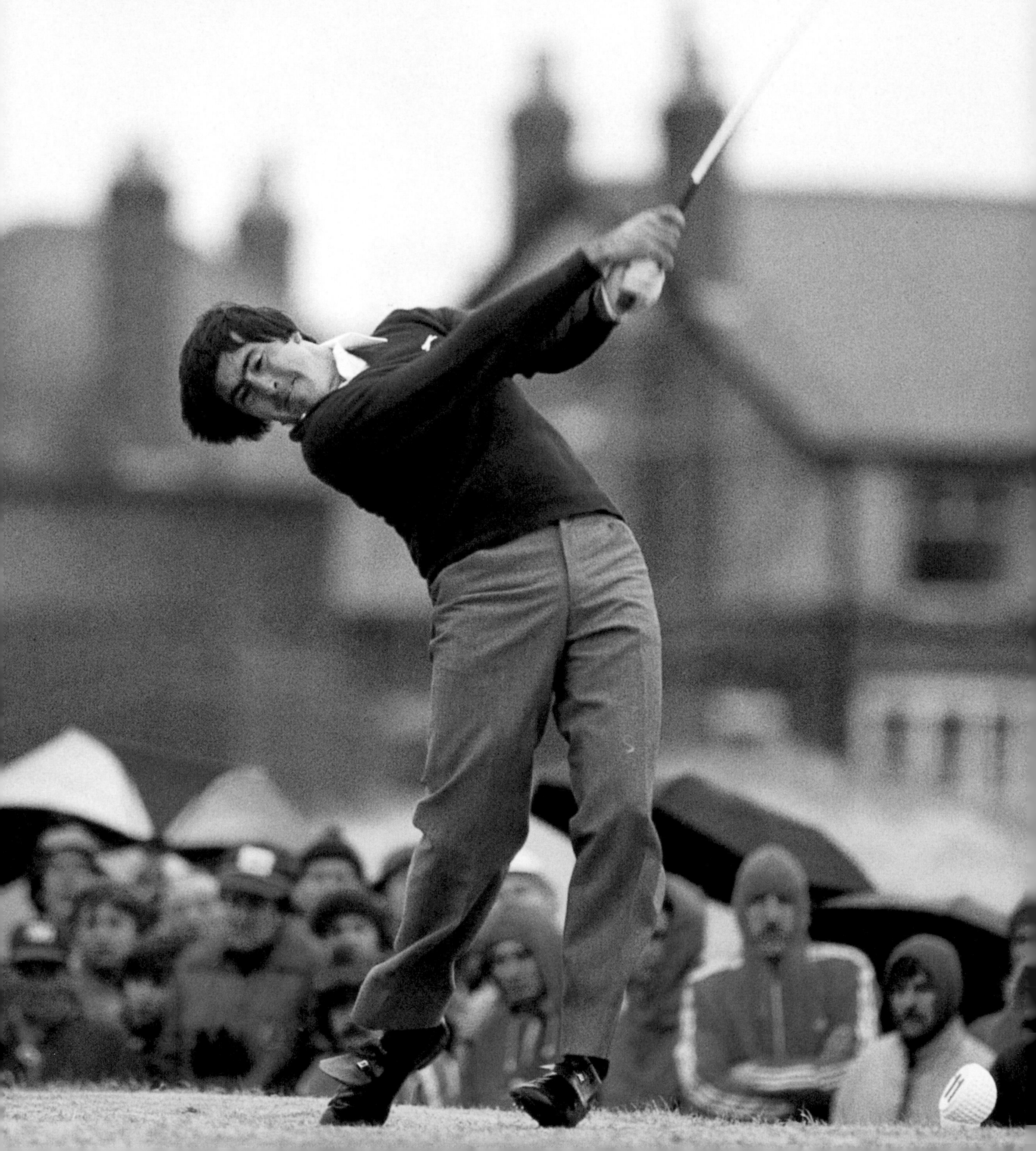

International Golf

Old Tom Morris would not know what to make of golf in modern Japan. The golf courses are mostly in the mountains, not by the sea. The greatest Japanese player, Masashi Ozaki, is half the size of a sumo wrestler, yet they call him "Jumbo." Japanese executives buy expensive clubs and shoes just to hit balls off mats at triple-tiered driving ranges. Professional golfers join training clubs called *gundans* and work out in the winter months at something akin to a baseball spring training camp. And although their moral and spiritual lives are governed by Buddhism and Shintoism, the Japanese play golf by the rules of the Royal and Ancient Golf Club of St. Andrews.

WINNING WAYS: Annika Sorenstam's methodical accuracy has made her the dominant player in woman's golf. By contrast, the forever-scrambling Seve Ballesteros (facing) won the 1979 British Open (and many other tournaments) with his spectacular improvisational play.

"All things have a history," explains Teruo Sugihara, the short-game wizard of Osaka. "Japan, golf, everything." The history of golf, however, is generally viewed from the perspective of the English speakers who invented the game. That leaves much of the story untold and gives a distorted picture of the game's development around the world.

Take Japan. The father of the Japanese game was Arthur Groom, an English trader who had offices in the port city of Kobe at the beginning of the twentieth century. Crowded Kobe offered little in the way of open space to Groom and his business friends, who had brought clubs and balls from England. There was, however, a modest mountain behind the city, Mount Rokko. Groom, a visionary, began to see Mount Rokko as a kind of linksland—the link, in this case, being between earth and sky. To the puzzlement of the Japanese, the Englishman and his friends climbed the mountain in 1901 and built a four-hole golf course. The design was crude, but the course had the virtue of inacces-

sibility. The golfers were carried up the mountain in sedan chairs, a backbreaking proposition that made the first Japanese caddies the strongest in the world.

Almost a century later, Sugihara reflected on the past and expressed concern, as old men do. "The young players today don't know the back story," he said at a tournament in Kyushu a few years ago. "They don't win with gratitude." Sugihara knew the back story because he was a *kan-reki*—literally, "return calendar." The Japanese calendar, like the Chinese, follows a twelve-year cycle—the Year of the Dog, the Year of the Rat, and so on—and one's sixtieth birthday marks the completion of five cycles. In olden times, disease and war permitted few Japanese to reach the age of sixty, so the kan-reki is treated as someone special, a person reborn. But Sugihara was more than a survivor. The son of a tenant farmer in Osaka, he had won sixty professional golf tournaments in Japan plus the 1969 Hong Kong Open—an amazing statistic when you consider that the Japanese Professional Golfers Association was not even founded until 1973, eighteen years after Sugihara became a golf pro.

Golf, too, is a kan-reki in Japan, in the sense that the game was born and then reborn. In its original incarnation, it was played by the Englishmen and a few rich Japanese and spread through the missionary zeal of Western course designers. The English architect H. C. Crane built the Naruo Golf Club at Inagawa in 1904. Another Englishman, C. H. Alison, visited the island nation in the 1930s and built several courses, including the Fuji Country Club and the Tokyo Golf Club. World War II erased these small inroads for golf: most courses were converted to farms and airfields.

In the postwar period, Japanese golfers learned the game by studying the pictures of Sam Snead and Ben Hogan in American instruction

HEADCOVERS: The original Japanese loopers were women, who wore long robes and straw sun hats. Below: Lian Huan Lo's near win at the 1971 British Open helped keep the porkpie hat in style.

HEADCOVERS: The original Japanese loopers were women, who wore long robes and straw sun hats. Below: Lian Huan Lo's near win at the 1971 British Open helped keep the porkpie hat in style.

books. The golf courses they played were second-rate, the competition insubstantial. "When I turned pro, there were only six tournaments and maybe 150 professionals," Sugihara recalled. "You survived by giving lessons and by winning money from the club members." In other words, Japanese golf in 1955 was much like American golf in 1905. That forty-year lag explains why, to the professionals of Sugihara's generation, it was important to "win with gratitude." It also goes a long way toward explaining why it took Japan three-quarters of a century to produce a player like the 1978 World Match Play champion Isao Aoki—the first Japanese golfer to win at the top level of international competition.

Japan is not the only country with an unappreciated back story. Only a Francophile, for instance, would recognize the name of Arnaud Massy, the Frenchman who won the 1907 British Open and then threw away the 1911 Open to Harry Vardon, uttering the timeless line, "I can't play zis damn game." Hardly anyone outside Argentina knows that anti-government terrorists once set off a bomb in the clubhouse of the Rosario Golf Club. ("Politics," muttered Roberto de Vicenzo, the club's onetime head pro and the 1967 British Open champion.)

Golf may have spread around the globe, but it is by no means universal. Put another way, there are golf countries and nongolf countries. It was no surprise when Greg Norman, an Australian, won the 1986 and 1993 British Opens; Peter Thomson, after all, had won five Opens for the Aussies between 1954 and 1965. It was big news, however, when Liang Huan Lo, a Formosan in a porkpie hat, finished second at Royal Birkdale in 1971, a stroke behind Lee Trevino. Similarly, winning nine major championships between 1959 and 1978 was deemed a stunning accomplishment on Gary Player's part, but not because he hailed from South Africa. After all, his countryman Bobby Locke, the portly Johannesburg golfer known as "Old Muffin Face," took four British Open titles between 1949 and 1957 and won eleven times in the United States in a four-year span. On the other hand, it seems extraordinary that the 1998 PGA and 2000 Masters champion Vijay Singh, an ethnic Indian, learned the game as a boy by hitting thousands of balls from the shade of a tree on the Fijian island of Viti Levu. And it is mind-boggling that Paraguay, a South American country with only three golf courses and perhaps 350 golfers, has produced Raul Fretes (who in one year, 1996, won the national championships of Peru, Uruguay, Chile, and China), Pedro Martinez (the leading money winner on the South American tour in 1994 and 1996), and Carlos Franco (a winner on the South American, Asian, Japanese, and U.S. tours and the PGA Tour rookie of the year in 1999). "I can't explain why we are such good players," said Fretes, who played on the Paraguayan team that defeated host Scotland in the 1993 Dunhill Cup. "Golf is not that popular in Paraguay, and most of us have never had lessons."

WILLS'S CIGARETTES.

ARNAUD MASSY.

Vive la Différence: Frenchman Arnaud Massy, a natural righty, played left-handed because a lefty set was all that was available in his hometown. In 1902, he went to Scotland, learned to play right-handed, and went on to make history for himself and France with his 1907 British Open victory.

The late flowering of certain nationalities in golf is easily explained. The game spread in the late eighteenth and nineteenth centuries as a direct consequence of British imperialism—meaning that it was most often glimpsed, by those colonized, from outside a wall or through a privet hedge. In India the Calcutta Golf Club was established in 1829 by the Scottish managers and engineers of the local jute mills. The Royal Bombay Golf Society got under way in 1843, and by 1892 there were enough *Times*-reading golfers in India to launch a national amateur championship—the first permanent golf competition outside the British Isles. Similar clubs and competitions sprang up in Ceylon, Burma, Singapore, and South Africa. In the New World, golf gained a foothold with the establishment of the Montreal Golf Club in 1873 (a full fifteen years before John Reid, the "father of American golf," teed it up in Yonkers). Eventually the Empire attracted golf professionals like

PRODIGIES: Round-cheeked Bobby Locke, a South African putting genius, won four British Opens from 1949 through 1957. He learned his "hooded blade" putting technique for maximum topspin from Walter Hagen. Facing: Peter Thomson, Australia's greatest international golfer, turned pro at nineteen in 1949 and went on to win five British Opens (including three in a row).

Sid and Jock Brews, who emigrated to South Africa and won twelve South African Opens between them from 1921 to 1952, and golf architects like Alister MacKenzie, who built courses in Australia, New Zealand, Canada, Argentina, Uruguay, and the United States. Even the Chinese—at least those who pulled weeds at the Hong Kong Golf Club (established in 1889)—could claim a passing familiarity with the game.

Early in the twentieth century, with golf on the rise around the world, it was only a matter of time before someone with deep pockets and a little imagination proposed a competition between nations. The first such encounter, between teams of amateurs sponsored by the Royal Canadian Golf Association and the United States Golf Association, took place in 1919 (in Canada) and in 1920 (in the United States); the United States won both times. On a separate front, USGA president George Herbert Walker, grandfather of President George Herbert Walker Bush, offered in 1921 to donate an International Challenge Trophy (instantly dubbed the "Walker Cup") and invited all interested countries to send teams to a competition. Only the British and Irish responded.

The first American Walker Cup team, captained by the 1910 U.S. Amateur champion William C. Fownes, played a one-day shakedown match against the British at Hoylake in 1921, winning 9–3. The following year, the R&A sent a team to the National Golf Links on Long Island, New York, for the first official match, and Fownes's team won again, 8–4. The United States, in fact, won nine straight matches before the team from Great Britain and Ireland won its first Walker Cup at St. Andrews in 1938. The series was suspended for nine years because of World War II, but upon resumption the United States continued its domination, losing only at St. Andrews in 1971 and at Atlanta in 1989. Since then, the two sides have achieved a competitive balance, winning three times each and making the Walker Cup, a biennial showcase for soon-to-be professional talent, the most appealing of international com-

Dai Rees as captain led the 1957 European Ryder Cup team to its first win since 1933.

petitions. A close second and third are the Curtis Cup, which since 1932 has pitted the women amateurs of the United States against those from Great Britain and Ireland, and the World Amateur Team Championship, begun in 1958, in which four-man amateur teams from around the world compete at stroke play for the Eisenhower Trophy.

While the amateurs of various countries pursue world domination with relatively little notice or antagonism, the professional competitions have come to resemble battles royal between teams of James Bond villains. The Ryder Cup, established in 1927 by the English seed merchant Samuel Ryder, bumbled along for decades as a biennial yawner between the best professional golfers of the United States and Great Britain. The two sides traded home victories in the first four matches, but the British managed only one victory and a tie between 1935 and 1977. "The Ryder Cup competitions, considering the wealth of colorful golfers who have been participants, have never been the events they should have been," wrote Herbert Warren Wind. "The PGA has shown less savvy than the USGA in mounting the matches held in America; and in handling their end of the deal, the British professionals' organization has not upheld the reputed British genius for administration." So amiable was the competition that players from the two sides often gathered after a day's matches to share a pint and swap stories. One favorite tale concerns Lee Trevino, who was so confident the night before his 1973 singles match with the English star Peter Oosterhuis that he told his teammates, "If I don't beat Oosterhuis,

I'll kiss every ass in the room." When Trevino trudged back to the U.S. locker room the next day after halving the match, he was met by the entire U.S. side sitting with their pants around their ankles.

To make a fairer fight of the Ryder Cup, the Brits asked for, and were granted, permission by the PGA of America to bring along a few friends from the Continent, starting in 1979. Over the next two decades, the European team turned the Ryder Cup into a trial by fire for the Americans. The Euros took the cup three straight times for their captain Tony Jacklin between 1985 and 1989; won it again for Bernard Gallacher in 1995; and then won it for the first time on the Continent for Seve Ballesteros in 1997. The best of the European players were

PASSAGE TO INDIA: A part of India's British colonial legacy, golf flourished for several decades and was popular in India many years before it came to America. Courses abound, including Ladakh (below), the venerable Royal Calcutta, and the thin-aired Gulmarg in Kashmir.

DIEHARDS: With a dedication only Hogan could equal, Fijian Vijay Singh (facing) has won the 1998 PGA and the 2000 Masters. Below: The nerve-wracking Ryder Cup brings out the best and worst of the competitive spirit: the victorious 1987 European squad kick-dances (top); the 1999 come-from-behind Americans rush the green.

Ballesteros, recovery artist and gamesman extraordinaire; Jose-Maria Olazabal, master of the short game and his emotions; Bernhard Langer, who fought off the yips by holding his putter against his left arm in the manner of a splint; Ian Woosnam, a scrappy Welshman no bigger than a mailbox; and the taciturn Nick Faldo, who would set records for Ryder Cup appearances (eleven) and points scored (twenty-five).

Along with high television ratings and sellout crowds, the European surge brought a change in tone. Strident nationalism and a win-at-all-costs mentality replaced the collegial atmosphere, turning the Ryder Cup into a pressure cooker for the players and an exercise in spin control for the captains. The extent of the pressure became apparent at Kiawah Island, South Carolina, in 1991, when the U.S. star and 1989 British Open champion Mark Calcavecchia walked along the beach, sobbing, after halving a singles match with Colin Montgomerie. The jingoism peaked on the final day of the 1999 matches in Brookline, Massachusetts, when the American players celebrated their dramatic Sunday comeback by running, jumping, and hugging each other before the deciding match had quite ended. The European captain Mark James later called it "the ugliest day in the game's history . . . the day the Ryder Cup about died of shame."

Bad blood notwithstanding, or perhaps because of it, the Ryder Cup is now the most anticipated, most watched, and most analyzed event in golf. So compelling is the format—three days of the world's best golfers playing for their countries instead of their bankbooks—that others have jumped in. In 1991 teams representing the Ladies Professional Golfers Association and the Women's Professional Golfers European Tour met at the

Fred Couples out of the rough at the ocean course at Kiawah in the 1991 Ryder Cup.

HOLE 15
468 YARDS
PAR 4

15

Lake Nona Club in Orlando, Florida, to launch their own biennial battle, the Solheim Cup. Four years later, the PGA Tour introduced the Presidents Cup, a United States v. International face-off scheduled for the fallow years of the Ryder Cup. Of the two copycats, the Solheim Cup seems the most likely to flourish, having perfected by 2000 the proven formula of gloating victors and resentful losers. The Presidents Cup provides a welcome showcase for underexposed talents like Shigeki Maruyama of Japan and Craig Perry of New Zealand, but faces a less certain future. "It's a great event," said the American tour star Davis Love III, "but it's not as exciting as the Ryder Cup."

GLOBAL REACH: The Shark, a.k.a. Greg Norman. Facing, clockwise: France's Jean Van de Velde at Carnoustie's 18th, where he snatched defeat from what looked like certain victory; two-time Masters winner Bernhard Langer has made a career out of battling the yips; Sergio Garcia and Karrie Webb, golf's new wunderkinder.

If at times America's best golfers seem cranky about the international cup craze, there is an explanation: they are no longer world-beaters. "Foreigners" won seven out of nine Masters championships between 1988 and 1996, and six out of seven U.S. Women's Open titles between 1995 and 2001. The top spot in the official world golf rankings was held in succession by a German (Bernhard Langer, winner of two Masters and practically every national title in Europe), a Spaniard (Seve Ballesteros, winner of five major championships), an Australian (Greg Norman, winner of fifty-six international tournaments and eighteen PGA Tour events), and a Brit (Nick Faldo, winner of three Masters and two British Open titles).

Globalization was even more pronounced on the LPGA Tour,

THE BIG EASY: A smooth swing and an easy manner are a winning combination for South Africa's Ernie Els, who has twice taken the U.S. Open.

with dominant performances turned in by Sweden's Annika Sorenstam (thirty-one tournament wins through 2001, plus three player-of-the-year trophies, three major titles, and the first competitive round of 59 in women's golf), Australia's Karrie Webb (twenty-five wins, five majors, twice player of the year), and South Korea's Se Ri Pak (three major titles in her first four full seasons). It was small consolation that most of these players moved to the United States to compete, practice, and spend their winnings.

The modern tour player, as often as not, is a man or woman with a fat passport. Thomas Bjorn, the Ryder Cupper from Denmark, lives in London and winters in Dubai, the vacation capital of the United Arab Emirates. Ernie Els, the two-time U.S. Open champion from South Africa, has a home in Capetown, another home at Wentworth outside London, and getaways in Orlando, Florida, and the Bahamas, just in case his plane lands at the wrong airport. Hundreds of lesser names plod year-round on the international treadmill, sipping Zambezi Lager at the Botswana Open, Inka Cola at the Peru Open, and Pocari Sweat at the Fancl Open in Okinawa. The best-adjusted of them adopt the roll-with-the-punches attitude of Sam Snead, who once asked a hotel man-

ager in the Belgian Congo whether he needed to worry about the mosquitoes. The manager replied, "Not if you've had spotted fever, malaria, and dengue fever."

Sometimes the foreign game looks like the American game seen through a prism. In South America, the tournament winner, like his North American counterpart, has his picture taken with a four-foot-wide cardboard check — the principal difference being the number of zeroes in front of the decimal. The Japanese tour mimics the American

JUMBOTRON: Once he was called "The Doug Sanders of golf," but now Masashi Ozaki is better known as "Jumbo." He started out as a professional baseball pitcher, but since 1969 his power game has dominated Japanese golf.

PLENTY OF ROLL: A pitch over an iceberg needs lots of spin. Golf in Greenland is usually limited to June through September.

tour in every respect, from gallery roping to electronic leader boards, but the ball makes a different sound when it falls into the cup—a musical ping instead of a rattle—and the bonneted female caddies replace the flagstick and then bow to the players waiting in the fairway.

The greater differences are in training and education. In Sweden, Australia, and South Korea, sports bureaucrats identify promising young golfers and put them in development programs. In Germany, new players have to pass a proficiency test to play on a championship course. At bottom, however, the game remains culturally transparent, adhering to the same rules and codes of conduct wherever it is played. Sugihara, the kan-reki, understood this, even if he sometimes worried that standards were slipping. "I want the Japanese player to understand why he can have this way of life," he said in Kyushu, thinking of Jumbo in his peacock outfits and the younger players with their Lexuses and Rolex watches. The view might be better from the mountaintop, in other words, but the achievement is in the climb.

The Caddiemaster

BY MICHAEL BAMBERGER

I was a looper in high school, and later I caddied on the pro golf tour, so when I joined an old-line Philadelphia club some years ago, I enjoyed a small measure of status with the caddiemaster, a gargantuan man, often grumpy, often cupping a cigarette, named Joe Smondrowski. Having some rapport with Joe was a good thing, because he was the most powerful and in-tim-idating person at the club. And he could make or break your golfing day. Joe controlled the first tee and all the places on the course where you thought you might insert your fast-moving self. You knew how you stood with Joe. If he didn't like you, he gave you a hard time. If he liked you, he gave you a harder time. How this made him endearing I don't know, but it did. In his years at the Philadelphia Cricket Club, Joe derived power from his knack for making people — members and guests — think they worked for him. This took a certain genius.

A visiting friend once showed up for the big July member-guest tournament, hoping to make a trip to the practice tee for a pre-round warm-up. The trip required a golf cart, and golf carts, of course, were the province of Joe. Joe detested giving up any of his carts. "Where's your member?" Joe barked at my friend when he asked for a buggy. In his fantasy life, my friend placed his right palm on his genitalia, gave a northward yank, and said, "Right here, buddy!" In real life, of course, he said nothing. He waited for his member in silence.

Joe had about a dozen regular caddies, double that in the summer months. His caddies would wait in the sun by an old garage, playing cards, reading newspa-pers, deconstructing Joe. They ranged in age consider-ably. Some were in high school and college, others in their sixties, having retired from the workaday world. Among the loopers there were golf bums, caddie lifers, societal dropouts, etc. Same as forever. Woody, who in his country-club youth played in the '64 U.S. Junior Amateur. Boxcar. Slider. In the good weather, they could make $80 a day, cash, $160 if they carried two bags twice. For a while there was a young woman, a delightful blonde who played field hockey and lacrosse at a local college. Joe never put her on my bag.

Joe would reserve his most enthusiastic caddies for me, in deference to my caddie experience. The truth is, all I've ever wanted from a caddie is the ability to dis-tinguish between uphill and downhill putts, but I'll take an overly involved caddie to a moping one anytime. In my early days at the club, Joe used to give me a caddie called Cobra. Cobra was an overweight red-haired kid in his midtwenties from a golfing family. As a caddie, he was consumed with helping his man shoot better scores. He was also a recovering alcoholic, a fact he discussed openly with me. Sometimes when I'd come in from a round, Joe would say to me, "Cobra save you a shot today?" Joe liked Cobra, not that Cobra ever knew. All part of the Joe method.

When my wife and I, as newlyweds, moved into our house, I hired Cobra for the day to help with the hauling. (I sought Joe's permission, of course. Joe was okay with it, as long as it wouldn't be on one of his busy days.) Cobra's work was excellent, and he put in a long day, grunting and sweating, interrupted only by a Burger King lunch. I wanted to pay Cobra generous-

ly for his work. I figured, had he carried two bags in the morning and two bags in the afternoon, a perfect payday would have been $88. I gave him $100. He looked neither pleased nor disappointed. Since that day, I've suffered with the idea that I underpaid him.

A couple of years later, Joe had Cobra on my bag when we came to the eighth hole at our club, a par-three playing 157 yards and into the breeze on this particular day. The hole was cut in a tricky position, on the right side of the green, on a knoll. There was no debate for me: it was a six-iron shot. I hit my six-iron a little over 160 yards in still conditions. As I put my hand on the six-iron, Cobra said, "No, no, no, not the six. It's a seven-iron." Now, I know my game well. I knew I'd have to smash a seven-iron to get the ball to the hole. It was not the correct club, but I took it anyhow, for two reasons. One, I still felt pangs of guilt that I may have underpaid him that day. Two, I didn't want to do anything to diminish his self-esteem as he continued his daily battle with sobriety. I distinctly remember taking the seven and saying to myself, "This one's for Cobra." The swing was sweet and solid, and the contact was pure, and the ball went in the hole, the only ace I've ever made. The word was out before I made it back to the clubhouse. Joe said to me, "Heard Cobra pulled a good stick for you on eight."

The loopers who studied closely the local caddying scene — like Cobra, or Woody — knew that Joe's model was a man named Mike Smith, the caddiemaster at Whitemarsh Valley, another club with old bones, separated from the Cricket Club by a housing development and a farm. Smith was a former Philadelphia cop who drove a big burgundy Cadillac, carried an enormous wad of cash in his back left pocket, and dressed with rare style. He'd occasionally work the staging area in white Foot-Joy teaching shoes, the kind club pros and old-school caddiemasters still wear, pink Sansabelt trousers, and a matching pink golf shirt with a collar so big and so stiff it seemed capable of flight.

Joe respected Smith's ride and stack and look, but what he admired most about Smith, what made Smith a legend, was his standing with his members and his caddies. The caddies respected him because he was loyal. He had one veteran caddie, Cigarman, who had served in World War II. Once, while walking past a stand of trees on the eleventh, Cigarman suddenly shouted to his group, "Sniper in the trees — hit the deck!" Cigarman slinked to the hole's border fence, took to his feet when he got under it, and went tearing down Thomas Road. The next day, Smith had Cigarman carrying a double, as if nothing had happened.

The members were indebted to Smith because he covered their gambling losses, which were sometimes considerable at Whitemarsh, a club with a large Irish-Catholic population where gambling, on the course and in the card room, was de rigueur. Smith's loans were interest-free, but he, of course, got his piece of the action in the end. When guys would come in, the first thing Smith would ask was, "Who got who?" Winners, typically, gave Smith a ten-spot. Losers always gave him the same, $10, or more. The joke at the club was that Smith was richer than most of the members. In his retirement, he was made a member.

In time, Joe bought himself the big Caddy (his was black) and got the big money-roll going (front right pocket for Joe). Joe's jumbo size ruled out dressing in Smith's color scheme, but he had the expensive Foot-Joy teaching shoes, and in cool weather he'd wear a proper Republican cardigan with the sleeves pushed up to his elbows, although he never looked quite like himself in it. Underneath the sweater, always, was a golf shirt with the Cricket Club emblem.

Every year, the day before Thanksgiving, Smith would come to the Cricket Club for a game. His host would be one of his former loopers. Smith would bring a small canvas bag with maybe ten clubs in it, lightening his caddie's load at the end of the season. Beside the great Michael Smith, Joe looked just a little less gargantuan. "How'd your year go, Mike?" Joe would ask earnestly. "Good, Joe, good," Mike would say. Joe would call out for his best caddie — Woody, more often than not — and watch in silence as the visiting caddiemaster would play his opening tee shot, march off the first tee and into the heart of Joe's course.

Woe, Woe, the Golf Pro

BY CURT SAMPSON

How was your round today, Mr. Updike? May I get your clubs for you, Mr. Welch? Yes, I'll make sure we clean them this time. The grooves, too, of course. Is that hook still bothering you, Mr. Jenkins? So you'd like to schedule another lesson? Sure, Easter Sunday, 10:00 A.M., would be fine. My six-year-old can find her own Easter eggs. Mr. Garrity, you'll be playing with Mr. McGrath today, would that be all right? No? Well, I'm sure we can arrange something else for a man of your wit and charm . . .

Forgive me. I learned sarcasm disguised by unnaturally agreeable chatter as a country club golf professional. Part athlete, part teacher, and part Eddie Haskell, the golf pro I was is the civilian I became. So if I seem fascinated by your vivid and detailed recap of your play on the back nine, particularly each shot and emotional surge of your nine on the thirteenth, rest assured that I'm faking it.

Like my paper wealth in the stock market, my sincerity died gradually, then suddenly. Mandatory butt-smooching wounded my ability to mean what I said. Working sixty hours a week while I perceived that the members worked sixty minutes made lying to myself and others still easier. Soon pleasant-sounding deceit became second nature and a valued skill, especially when your wife called the pro shop. "Yes, Mrs. Smith, Mr. Smith just left," I'd say, sounding like a bartender.

In this way, we club pros became intimates with our betters. We were keepers of secrets for people we saw at their worst, corporate titans humbled by their quest to win B flight. Some of you we got to know entirely too well.

The bête noire for my friend Jimmy, a former club pro from Georgia, was a ten-handicap lawyer who put in almost as many hours at the club as he did. "I was closin' up one night, and saw the light on in the sauna. And there was Loophole, just passed out and naked as he could be. Spread-eagled. So I pulled him out, put him in a chair, and he begs me for a drink. So I pour him a glass of gin and leave. Next morning, Loop's still in that chair, just like before. Naked, snoring, his head thrown back and his legs wide open. Lord."

Another club, another member, another pro: after a wild night of passion with a girl he met at a wedding reception, the young assistant has concerns about his reproductive health. He confides in the club president, an ingratiating man and a physician. Days later, the popular pro is fired because the board suddenly has questions about his morals.

The drunk and the devious were difficult for any of us in the country club to handle, but I was also perfectly lousy at the most routine interaction. "How did you play today, Mr. Brown?" I'd ask, as custom dictated, hoping only for a number and a summary: "Eighty-eight. Can't putt." Too often, however, I'd get trapped by a soliloquy. But one pro I worked for always handled this situation beautifully.

Pro: So how was it today, Jim?

Golfer: The wind began to blow from a new quarter, the southwest, I think, when I teed off on One, so I decided to hit a three-wood. Thrice I inhaled the pine-scented air before I addressed the ball . . .

Pro: [*interrupting*] Christ, Jimmy, would you at least start on the back nine?

If that didn't stop Mr. Boring, the pro might loudly observe that 95 percent of people don't care what you shot. And the other 5 percent wish it had been higher.

Golfer: [*oblivious*] . . . and hit my three-wood a bit on the heel. I had about 148 to the hole, down-wind, but the wind died, so I decided to take off my sweater . . .

An ironic aspect of the golf pro's lament is that no one is likely to attend to it except other golf pros. The club environment looks luxurious and decadent, with carpets so thick and clothes so nice that those outside the life just don't want to hear any complaining. They think golf pros wear Polo and play golf all the time.

"That may be what bothers me most about this job," admitted an assistant pro in Dallas. "Not the people who bitch, or the fact that I could make more money waiting tables. It's that people assume you play golf every day. Bullshit. What if you're married and have children? You never get weekends or holidays off. So after fifty or sixty hours here, when it's time to punch out, I'm gone."

Thus, golf pros become like diabetics standing outside a candy store. They get your clubs, and sell you a glove and some balls, get your foursome on the tee, and watch you hit. And though they went into the business because they love the game, they don't get to play it much. What they do instead is teach, which can be a rich, rewarding experience if the student improves. Or a frustrating, embittering fiasco if he does not.

My experience as an instructor may be typical. As the junior member of the staff, I was given the twice-weekly junior clinic, consisting of two dozen kids of varying age, skill, and enthusiasm. Clueless about how to teach, I merely told them, "Here, do it like this," and demonstrated. Monkeys saw, monkeys did. The juniors improved that summer, and by fall I was promoted to the adult beat. "Here, do it like this," I said again. "Like this?" No . . . Hamstrung by intellect, the mature human is less able to imitate. Worse, the grown-ups liked to debate. "But Dan told me I need to stand closer to the ball, not farther away," was a classic. "Jack Nicklaus always raises his right elbow up on the backswing." And I heard more times than I can count "That's not what *Golf Magazine* says." Many students actually brought the latest magazines to their tutorials, wishing only for their instructor to read aloud the captions under the swing sequence photographs while they hit striped golf balls into the humid air.

Three times I've joined country clubs, and three times I've resigned. I have no doubt that my years as a golf pro are to blame for my failure to blend, my utter inability to do the club thing. During my member tenures, I'd hang around the bag room or the pro shop, maybe help pick up the balls on the practice range, gossip with the assistants about the other members, and drink and play golf with the staff.

Perhaps I'm an old dog unable to learn a new trick. Perhaps I admire the perseverance of the golf pro, and his love for the pure game of golf.

And he loves you, too. Honest! Would your golf pro lie?

chapter 6

Television

Y ou could see Arnold Palmer's head and shoulders over the brow of the hill as he came into camera range on the fifteenth hole at Augusta National. Then you saw him to the waist, and then to the knees, hitching up his trousers and flipping his cigarette aside, a portrait of purposeful agitation. It was the final round of the 1959 Masters, and Palmer, the tournament leader and defending champion, was trying to recover from a triple bogey on the twelfth hole. Frank Chirkinian, sitting in a CBS truck parked off the course, watched on a bank of black-and-white television monitors, his right hand hovering over the button that would change the picture beamed to a national audience of about three million homes. Chirkinian's training told him to switch to a shot

THE FACE THAT LAUNCHED A MILLION SLICES: More than anyone else, Arnold Palmer made golf a popular spectator sport, inspiring hackers everywhere to take up the game. Above: A view from inside the truck.

of somebody hitting a golf ball. His instincts told him to stay with the greenskeeper's son from Latrobe, Pennsylvania. Decades later, Chirkinian would remember it as the moment television golf came of age.

Palmer fought like a hooked fish that day. After his 6 on the twelfth, he fought back with birdies on Thirteen and Fifteen, but he missed a gut-wrenching two-foot putt on Seventeen, drawing gasps and moans from the gallery. Meanwhile, undemonstrative Art Wall Jr.—known in television trucks as "the ribbon clerk" because he looked like he belonged behind a small-town notions counter—birdied five of the last six holes to edge Palmer by a shot.

Wall got the green jacket, but in living rooms and bars and coun-

try clubs across the land, viewers connected with the monochrome image of "Arnie." "The cameras capture the essence of a person," Chirkinian said. "They either love you or hate you, and they loved Arnold." What those long-legged buckets of ground glass, tubes, and electrical wire saw in Palmer was a fighter, a brawler. "Hitch up the pants, roll up the sleeves, and dive in," said Terry Jastrow, who directed and produced ABC golf telecasts for twenty-two years. "There's something fundamentally American about that."

The early golf telecasts were crude—no color, no hand-held cameras, no sound of the ball rattling in the cup. The magic was not in the technology, but in Palmer. He had the stage actor's sense of nuance, the ability to project a full emotional range over distance by posture and gesture alone. "Arnold played to the camera a little bit," Jastrow said. "He walked to the best side of the green. His image would usually be framed correctly for my needs."

Palmer was more than an image, of course. After dropping out of Wake Forest University, he won the 1954 U.S. Amateur and then found immediate success as a pro, winning the Canadian Open as a rookie in 1955. His Masters victory in 1958 was the first of seven major titles in a seven-year span. When Palmer wasn't storming from behind to win a major (as he did in the 1960 U.S. Open at the Cherry Hills Country Club, firing a final-round 65), he was storming from ahead to lose (as he did at the 1966 U.S. Open, where he blew a seven-stroke final-round lead and lost in a playoff to Billy Casper). Between 1960 and 1963, Palmer won twenty-seven PGA events and two British Opens, an average of better than seven wins a year. He was "the King," and the boisterous battalion of fans that followed him was "Arnie's Army." There was

THE PRODUCER: Frank Chirkinian favored personality—read Arnie—over equal coverage, to golf's lasting benefit. Standard procedure now is to stick with the leaders—unless Tiger is playing.

Passing the jacket from Arnie to Jack at Augusta in 1965.

even an "Air Force." If he finished poorly in a tournament or missed the cut, Palmer, a licensed pilot, would take to the sky in his private plane for a see-you-next-week buzz of the eighteenth fairway—preferably when his pal Chris Schenkel of ABC was on the air.

"At first, television was an intrusion," Palmer says, recalling golf's skirmishes with the new medium in the 1950s. "I made a few speeches in those days about the fact that if the guys only realized how important television was to the game, they wouldn't be upset. But I can remember a couple of times when *I* got upset, when I was delayed or distracted by the technicians." A cartoon of the 1950s showed a golfer putting while a man standing with a microphone at the edge of the green murmured, "He's lining up the putt, he's ready to take the putter back, now he's glaring angrily in my direction. . . ." Some years later, on the *CBS Golf Classic,* the man with the microphone was the former U.S. Open champion Ken Venturi, who asked Miller Barber about his lie. "Lie? I've got no f——ing lie," Barber fumed. "I don't even have a f——ing shot!"

One of the problems of early television was that it often wasn't television at all, but film. The pioneering golf series of the 1950s, *All-Star Golf,* used equipment better suited to the soundstage than a 150-acre golf course. The cameras had to be moved for every shot, the light had to be just so, and it was a good day if the director got nine holes in the can. Another black-and-white series, *Challenge Golf,* employed Palmer and Gary Player as both players and announcers, leading to some unprofessional but endearing commentary. ("Gary has hit a beautiful shot, a high shot, and it's drawing toward the flag and landing, and it's about 40 feet short of the hole, and he'll have a very long putt from there to the hole, about 40 feet . . .") When it *was* television, it could be exciting. The very first nationally televised golf tournament, the 1953 World Championship at Tam O'Shanter Country Club, ended spectacularly when Lew Worsham holed a 121-yard wedge shot for a one-stroke victory over Chandler Harper.

The role of the announcers was problematic from the start. "Television is, by comparison with radio, a pushover," wrote Henry Longhurst, a British writer turned golf commentator. "In television . . . you can always intersperse what Sydney Smith, referring to the loquacious Macauley's conversation at dinner, called 'brilliant flashes of silence.'" Unfortunately, some early not-so-silent moments in televised golf tended to be less than brilliant, as when analyst Byron Nelson told commentator Schenkel, "Chris, the boys are hitting the ball longer now because they're getting more distance." The former PGA champion Bob Rosburg became notorious as a course reporter for whispering to his

HIS KINGDOM FOR A BIRDIE: The body English, the smile, the near make, the bold play—and Arnie's Sunday charge at the 1960 U.S. Open—made him the game's reigning superstar.

audience that a player "had no shot" from behind a tree or from under the lip of a bunker, only to have the player whip his ball onto the green and snug against the flagstick.

Fortunately, when the announcers got in trouble, they usually had the charismatic Palmer to rescue them. With Palmer as pilot and television as his craft, golf took off. The number of American golf courses and golfers roughly doubled between 1960 and 1990, while tournament purses, inflated by television revenues and corporate sponsors, soared. As had happened with Francis Ouimet (and would later be the case with Tiger Woods), even Americans with only a passing interest in sports followed the fortunes of the young man from Latrobe. "I was raised in a steel town, a coal-mining area," Palmer explained late in his career. "I played golf, but very few people in the town really knew anything about it. That's where television really had a tremendous impact on the game. It took golf into the coal mines, the steel mills, into every business and walk of life."

It soon became clear that television was not a tide that lifted every boat. Ben Hogan, an icon in still photography, seemed less monumental on television and more of a Texas sourpuss—a runty one at that. Sam Snead, on the other hand, translated well to the small screen, especially on *All-Star Golf* and *Shell's Wonderful World of Golf,* where his coconut-straw hat, graceful swing, and southern drawl made icebound northern golfers want to call their travel agents. Gene Littler, with an equally beautiful swing and wins in the 1961 U.S. Open and twenty-eight other PGA events, made almost no impression on the screen. It was the same for most of the other golf stars of the period. Julius Boros, the easygoing winner of the 1952 and 1963 U.S. Opens, looked ursine on the tube. The two-time U.S. Open champion Cary Middlecoff, a former dentist, was numbing. Even

the 1958 PGA champion Dow Finsterwald, a mustachioed gambler and gamesman of the old school, came across on TV as your Uncle Dow at the breakfast table, sucking on his teeth while reading the newspaper.

Consider, then, the plight of the twenty-two-year-old Jack Nicklaus. Heavy and grim, the Ohio State University graduate cut his hair in a military-style flattop and wore clothes that looked as if they had been ironed only once, by J. C. Penney. When "Fat Jack" beat the beloved Arnie in a playoff to win the 1962 U.S. Open at Oakmont Country Club, the camera blinked and the golf world gagged. A year later, when Nicklaus won the Masters and the PGA Championship, the typical golf fan wanted to cry. Nicklaus was "the bully on the block who owned the bat and the ball, had the first car, got the first girl," wrote William Price Fox in *Golf Digest*. "And when he sliced off tackle for twelve yards it always took three of us to drag him down. He was too much."

Nicklaus, in the age of television, had two choices: stay the course and wind up like the rotund and devout Billy Casper, whose three major championships and forty-eight other tour wins excited people less than the fact that he ate buffalo meat . . . or become somebody else. With the encouragement of his wife Barbara, Nicklaus became somebody else. He lost weight. He threw away his golf caps and let his hair grow out in soft blond bangs. He slipped into the paisleys and plaids of golf's polyester era. When he holed a long putt or won a tournament, he lifted his putter and smiled. When he went to the press tent for

GOLDEN BEAR: Another side of Jack Nicklaus. In the 1970s and early 1980s, Jack loosened up. He let his hair grow and played to the crowds, but he was as prepared to win as ever. Bottom: Jack's notes on his 1963 Augusta scorecard.

interviews, he *talked*—in a squeaky voice, to be sure, but long and well. If, as Chirkinian argued, the camera captured the essence of a person, Nicklaus proved the corollary: that the camera could be wooed and won over.

With his image altered, Nicklaus emerged as a fan favorite—"Fat Jack" became the "Golden Bear." Tournament galleries marveled at his length off the tee, his brute strength from the rough, and the height of his long-iron shots, which let him attack flags that other players could go for only with a wedge. When Nicklaus won the 1965 Masters, Bobby Jones said, "Jack is playing an entirely different game—a game I'm not even familiar with." Nicklaus's real strength, however, was course management. More than any player before or since, Nicklaus thought his way around a golf course, refusing to execute a shot or stroke a putt until he had considered all the options and performed a cost-benefit analysis. "Most of the time he plays with the timidity of a middle-aged spinster walking home through a town full of drunken sailors," wrote the British golf writer Peter Dobereiner, "always choosing the safe side of the street." That side of the street, it turned out, was where you found the trophy shops. Nicklaus won a record eighteen major championships— six Masters, five PGA Championships, four U.S. Opens, and three British Opens. He was also runner-up in an incredible nineteen majors between 1960 and 1986.

Having good television personalities didn't help Palmer and Nicklaus get the ball into the hole, but it enhanced an increasingly important part of tour life: marketing. Sports personalities had long been in demand as endorsers

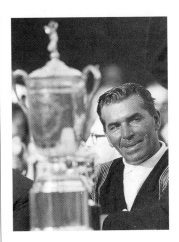

BUILT TO LAST: At forty-three, Julius Boros won the 1963 U.S. Open, becoming the second oldest winner after Ted Ray. Inspired by this middle-aged success, Boros became a pioneer of the Senior Tour. Below: Mark McCormack with the three golfers who became the foundation of his empire.

UP AND DOWN: In the 1964
U.S. Open, dehydrated
Ken Venturi played Satur-
day's 36-hole final round
and came from six back
to beat Tommy Jacobs and
Arnold Palmer. Facing:
Watson's legendary chip-
in at Pebble Beach's 17th;
the shot broke a subpar
deadlock with Nicklaus,
enabling Watson to win
the 1982 U.S. Open.

of products; Babe Ruth is remembered for the Baby Ruth candy bar created in his honor, but the Yankees slugger also pitched hardware, Florida real estate, and a dozen other products. In golf, the dollar parade started with Harry Vardon, who endorsed the Vardon Flyer golf ball; it passed through Bobby Jones, who starred in a series of Hollywood-produced instruction films in the 1930s; and it wound up at the corner of Main Street and Wall Street with Palmer and Nicklaus, who would become the two most marketable athletes in the world. Through advertising, consumers learned that the King drank Coca-Cola, smoked L&M cigarettes, and dressed his hamburgers with Heinz catsup, while the Golden Bear wore Hathaway shirts, Bostonian shoes, and suits by

Hart Schaffner & Marx. Palmer pitched cars for Lincoln-Mercury and lubricated the airwaves with folksy commercials for Pennzoil, taking care not to get any on his Rolex watch. Nicklaus drove a Pontiac, paid his hotel bills with an American Express card, sprayed his lawn with Fertigrow, and barbecued on a Magic Chef grill.

Both golfers complained about the distractions of commerce — "Posing with fashion models for hours at a time was a hell of a lot harder than I imagined it would be," Palmer wrote in his autobiography — but both pursued business opportunities as feverishly as they sought birdies. They were aided in the hunt by Mark McCormack, a Cleveland lawyer and Yale Law School graduate who was hired in 1959 by Palmer to manage his business affairs. With Palmer as his

Welshman Ian Woosnam
after winning the 1995
Masters.

DREAMS SO REAL: Curtis
Strange fantasized about
winning a U.S. Open ever
since he was a little boy
playing on the Virginia
course his father owned.
In 1988 his dream came
true at The Country Club.
He did it again the next
year at Oak Hill (below).

first and defining client (and with Nicklaus in the fold for a decade), McCormack founded International Management Group (IMG), the biggest and most powerful sports marketing and management company in the world. By the year 2000, IMG had offices on six continents, represented clients as diverse as Tiger Woods, Queen Elizabeth, and Pope John Paul II, and had expanded into event management and literary agenting. (When asked whether McCormack's outfit is worth the healthy commissions it charges, the English golfer Tony Jacklin said, "It's a matter of getting a percentage of millions or of thousands.")

Thanks to television exposure, the touring professionals no longer had to supplement their incomes by holding club jobs. But this otherwise happy turn of events created a rift within the Professional Golfers Association. The club pros, who toiled on the lesson tees and sold goods in pro shops, came to resent the glamorous touring pros, who played to

cheering crowds and got free clothing and equipment from the manufacturers. The tournament players, in turn, bridled at the PGA's onerous membership rules and control of television revenues. In 1968 a group of unhappy touring pros that included Nicklaus, Frank Beard, and two former PGA champions, Doug Ford and Gardner Dickinson, formed the Association of Professional Golfers and hired the PGA tournament director Jack Tuthill to organize a competing tournament schedule. Palmer—as disenchanted as the "radicals" with the PGA bureaucracy, but less willing to blow everything up—pushed for the creation of a Tournament Players Division within the PGA. After months of debate, the Palmer faction prevailed. Joe Dey, the longtime executive director of the USGA, was hired as commissioner of the Tournament Players Division, and the touring pros and club pros went their separate ways. The Tournament Players Division eventually dropped all ties with the newly named PGA of America and became a free standing, not-for-profit corporation: the PGA Tour.

To golf fans, the impact of tour politics was minimal; they saw the same players at the same tournaments on the same small screen. To the players, however, the impact was huge. Under Dey—and later under one of their own, the imperious tour-journeyman-turned-commissioner Deane Beman—the PGA Tour joined with corporate America and the television networks in an arrangement that entertained millions. The new tour enriched not just the golf stars of the seventies, like Johnny Miller and Tom Weiskopf, but players well down the money list.

RHINESTONE COWBOYS: Johnny Miller dismantled Oakmont with a 63 to win the 1973 U.S. Open. That same year, Tom Weiskopf beat Miller for the British Open. Both favored loud clothing and torrid play.

The cameras, meanwhile, continued to lavish their affection on a favored few. Chi Chi Rodriguez, a featherweight Puerto Rican with a million finesse shots in his bag, grabbed airtime by performing a sword dance whenever he made an important putt. Lee Trevino, a hustler from San Antonio, parlayed a thrift-shop swing and a "Super Mex" act into six major championships and a network variety show. When the cutups weren't in contention, the cameras searched for the tried and true: Palmer, with his whiplash follow-through, his eyes tracing the ball's flight with the worried intensity of a hawk, and Nicklaus, with his slow, fastidious pre-shot routine, mentally assembling the shot the way an assassin in a movie puts together his rifle. "ABC depends too much

on star power," groused Frank Chirkinian (of all people). "They follow Nicklaus everywhere, even when he's not in contention."

In the spring of 1986, a forty-six-year-old Nicklaus made ABC look prescient, although it was Chirkinian and CBS who benefited. Years past his prime, the Golden Bear shot 30 on the last nine holes of the final round of the Masters to win the green jacket for the fifth and last time. "Here was Nicklaus, in one swell swoop, reaching down from another era and snatching a major championship from the reigning czars of this one," wrote Rick Reilly in *Sports Illustrated*. A highlight of the final round was Nicklaus's eagle on the par-five fifteenth hole—the same hole where Palmer, almost two decades before, had grown from a small figure to an international icon on screens across the land. This time, with Chirkinian again calling the shots from a CBS trailer, the cameras came together on Nicklaus and his eagle putt. You got the parabolic path of slow-moving ball on well-mowed grass, the eyes of the man following the ball, the full-throated roar of the crowd when the ball toppled into the hole. Nicklaus thrust his putter in the air, and the slanting sun lit the club, his hair, his smile . . . history.

Tiger Woods after winning
the 1997 Masters.

LEADERS

THRU 17

WOODS	18
ROCCA	4

HOLE	1	2	3	4	5	6	7	8	9	10	11	12	13	14	15	16	17	18
PAR	4	5	4	3	4	3	4	5	4	4	4	3	5	4	5	3	4	4
15 WOODS																		
6 ROCCA																		
5 STANKOWSKI																		
4 KITE T																		
4 WATSON, T.																		
3 SLUMAN																		
1 LOVE																		
2 LANGER																		
2 COUPLES																		
0 TOLLES																		

The Tour
According
to Tiger

BY JOHN FEINSTEIN

On a cool spring morning in March 1998, Ben Brundred finally got the Call. He had thought it might come and had calculated the chances over and over again. When he hung up the phone, he walked out of his office, a huge smile on his face, and told everyone the news: "He's coming."

No one had to ask Brundred, then the tournament director for the Kemper Open, what he meant, or who "he" was. For anyone who has worked in professional golf since August 1996, there is only one "he": Eldrick T. Woods, better known as Tiger, no last name required. For Brundred—or any tournament director on the PGA Tour—getting the Call means that his life and his tournament will never be quite the same.

Woods has changed golf forever with his extraordinary accomplishments. But he has also changed golf in ways that don't show up in TV ratings or newspaper headlines. He has, for all intents and purposes, divided the PGA Tour into two tiers: Tiger weeks and non-Tiger weeks. A Tiger week is so different from a non-Tiger week that you might think two different sports are being played.

It isn't as if Woods is golf's first superstar. But no one, not Nicklaus and his eighteen majors or Palmer and his unmatched charm and charisma, has been Tiger. He's an icon of the twenty-first century, a media age when every movement, every utterance, every misstep of our celebrities is chronicled, replayed, and rehashed for days, weeks, and months. He is also both a tool and a beneficiary of commercial packaging that is unparalleled in the history of our planet. If you watch television for more than fifteen minutes at a time, you are going to see Tiger's smiling visage, selling golf clubs, golf balls, cars, credit cards, magazines, and, in his most recent multimillion-dollar deal, Mickey Mouse.

There isn't a three-year-old in America who doesn't know who Tiger is. What's more, at least for now he doesn't have a Great Rival. Hogan had Snead and Nelson; Palmer had Nicklaus and Player; Nicklaus had Watson; Norman had Ballesteros and Faldo—who were actually better players but never marketed into stardom the way Norman was.

Until Tiger's arrival, tournament directors scrapped and fought over Norman and Fred Couples and Nick Price and Davis Love III. They still try to entice these players to play in their event, whether by giving them an annual Christmas present, tickets to local ballgames, a one-week deal on a three-bedroom condo, or by standing on the range at another tournament pleading. But now every big name in the game can show up, and there's only one question a tournament director is going to be asked by the local media: "Is Tiger playing?" And if the answer is no, there's a follow-up question: "Do you think he might play next year?"

For the tour, this is a good-news/bad-news joke. The good news is that Tiger likes to play. When Norman and Price were the number-one players in the world BT (Before Tiger), each usually played only fifteen PGA Tour events a year—the minimum required to retain tour membership. Norman is Australian, and Price is from Zimbabwe; both liked to jump on their private jets and fly overseas to play because overseas tournaments are allowed to pay appearance fees and PGA Tour events are not.

Tiger will certainly fly for the money, too. Early in 2001, he played in Dubai for an appearance fee of $2 million. But he also plays a lot on the PGA Tour. In 2000, he teed it up in the United States twenty times. That's the good news. The bad news is that twenty-three other tournament directors had to face the "Why no Tiger?" question.

The Kemper Open, played outside of Washington, D.C., for twenty-two years, has always drawn large crowds. It is generally held one to three weeks before the U.S. Open, and the quality of its field varies, depending on the date. In 1998 the date was two weeks prior to the Open, and Brundred thought this would be his chance.

"We all know Tiger doesn't usually like to play the week before a major," Brundred said. "But he does like to play two weeks out more often than not. We had our fingers crossed."

As soon as the Call came, Brundred's office took on the look of a command center anticipating the arrival of the President. Lengthy meetings were held with the local county executive, the police chief, private security officials, representatives of the FAA, the chamber of commerce, and nearby hotel managers. There were to be no glitches from the moment Tiger's plane touched down until the moment the wheels went up six days later.

No golfer in history has been surrounded by security the way Tiger is. In fact, the PGA Tour had to take steps early in his career to get the security people to back off. At one event, Tiger's people announced that the locker room was closed while Tiger was inside. They kept out not only the media but other players.

One of the tour's media officials was quite blunt with Tiger's people: "The locker room out here has been open for Palmer, for Nicklaus, for Watson," he said. "It's open for this kid, too. He's not the fifth Beatle."

Not then he wasn't. Now the Beatles would play backup for him. As a result, everywhere Tiger goes the security is sure to follow.

PGA Tour locker rooms are, generally speaking, fairly relaxed places, and members of the media are made to feel welcome by most players. But when Tiger walks in, you can feel the tension mount. It isn't because Tiger himself is tense; he's more comfortable in the locker room environment now than he was when he first came on the scene, and his relationship with his fellow players has greatly improved. But Tiger in the locker room isn't like anyone else in the locker room. He's not one of the guys — no number-one player ever is — and he never lingers. He comes in with a purpose and leaves with a purpose. His presence never goes un-

noticed. Players often joke that the weeks Tiger plays, the tour becomes the TGA Tour.

No one is more aware of all this than PGA (TGA) Tour Commissioner Tim Finchem. Those tournament directors who do not get Tiger in their field are constantly demanding that Finchem convince him to diversify his schedule. In 2000, however, Finchem's occasional pleas to Woods to play a few places he hadn't played before backfired when Tiger publicly complained that Finchem talked to him only when he wanted him to play in another event. Finchem probably won't do that again anytime soon.

And those who buy tickets for the Kemper Open are still not likely to see Woods in their midst anytime soon. He never did make it to the Kemper back in 1998. The week before, playing at the Memorial (Nicklaus's tournament, which he plays in every year), Tiger felt a slight twinge in his back. He wasn't taking any risks two weeks before the U.S. Open. As Brundred sat in his office on Monday afternoon, making final arrangements for Tiger's impending arrival, his assistant walked in to say that the Man himself was on the phone.

At that moment, Brundred was with Jim Kemper, CEO of the Kemper Open, and Steve Lesnick, the tournament's head of marketing. They all looked at one another. "Probably needs more tickets or something," Brundred said, trying to stay calm.

He picked up the phone. Kemper and Lesnick knew right away the call wasn't about tickets. Brundred went very pale. "I understand, Tiger, I appreciate you making the call yourself," they heard him say. "I hope you feel better real soon."

Realizing what was happening, Lesnick began waving his arms to get Brundred's attention. He was mouthing something, but in the state he was in, Brundred couldn't read Lesnick's lips. He hung up.

"You heard?" he said.

Both men nodded sadly.

"Steve," Brundred asked, "what were you trying to tell me while I was talking to him?"

"I was trying to tell you," Lesnick said, "to get him to commit for next year."

Waiting Game

BY CHANG-RAE LEE

It is 3:30 A.M. on a cool June morning, and I am in Bethpage, Long Island. My home is forty miles away, clear on the other side of New York City, in suburban New Jersey. But here I am alone, and not completely unhappy. I am lying down in the back of my old Honda station wagon, waiting for the man to drive down from the clubhouse and hand out the numbered tickets.

They're going to hold the U.S. Open here, on the Black Course (the one I'm aiming to play in the morning), and you can't get a tee time the normal way anymore, which is to call on the telephone reservation system. I've been trying for weeks, but I don't have an auto-redialer. If the line isn't busy, the earliest time I can get is a 3:50 P.M. slot, which means it's unlikely I'll finish the round before dark. Even with the five courses here at Bethpage State Park, there are too many golfers in the megalopolis. They cram us in, and it takes over five hours to play, sometimes six.

This afternoon I called and happened to talk to a real person. He told me the best way to get one of the walk-up slots is to camp out the night before, the way people do for Bruce Springsteen tickets.

"So I just come and wait in my car?"

"Yeah, you'll see."

"But what time should I get there?"

"It's up to you."

"What time would *you* get there?"

"I'm not a golfer."

"Let's say you were."

"Maybe midnight, one. Some guys come earlier. Hey, it's up to you."

After dinner I told my wife, Michelle, of my plans, and she gazed at me with gravest love and pity, as if she had just realized the full extent of my Golf Problem, how deep it ran and how dark. She could only faintly nod as I explained that this was an opportunity, the only surefire way to experience a classic layout from the elegant, expressive hand of A. W. Tillinghast, because who knew when I'd ever be invited to Winged Foot or Baltusrol. And then, besides being at one of the nation's temples of truly public golf, where the fee is a most plebian $32, I'd be playing the very track Tiger and Vijay and Sergio would be playing in the Open, hitting (in the broadest sense) the same drives and approaches, the same chips and putts.

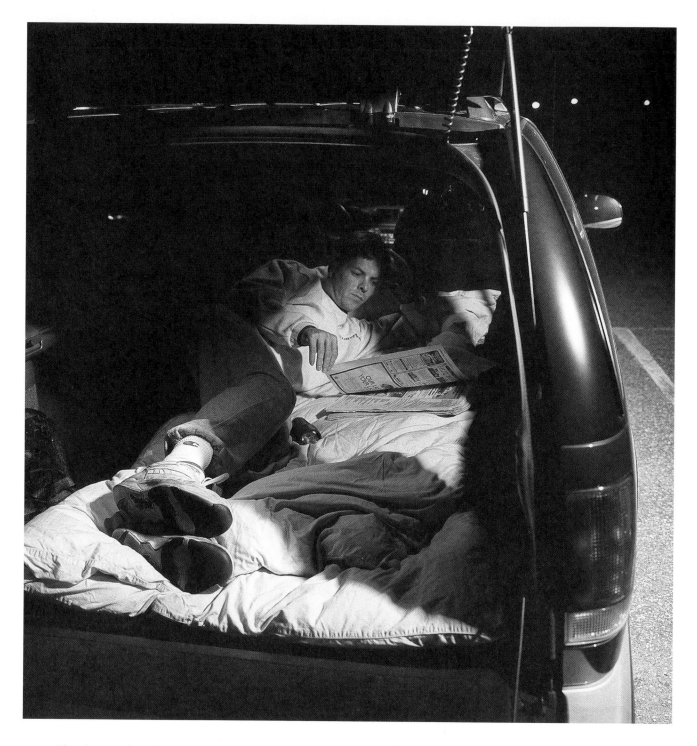

She shrugged and left me to my planning. I timed it so I'd get to the course just around midnight, which, sad to say, is well past my usual bedtime. I'd fall dead asleep and power-nap until 4:30, when the man supposedly came out. I'd snag my early time, then power-nap again, until the dawn broke and I'd head to the range for a bucket of balls and a big coffee and prepare myself to bring the lengthy and magnificent Black Course to its knees as the dew burned off the gleaming, majestic fairways.

A fine stratagem indeed, but now, in the parking lot, I am having trouble with the sleep part. The seats are folded down, and if I lie diagonally, I can almost stretch out fully. Beside me is my golf bag, the two of us scrunched together in the narrow space between the wheel wells, so that if I shift, the irons *click-clack* and the head covers tickle my face. I have brought everything I need — or at least, what I thought I would need — for a good night's rest: (1) down sleeping bag, from long-ago camp days, moldy-smelling in the seams; (2) corduroy couch pillow, from where, I don't know; (3) earplugs; (4) an exhaustive history of the Pacific air war during World War II; (5) a fresh pint of Dewar's.

None of the above is of much use, however, because what I imagined would be a serene encampment of slumbering golfers is in reality a drive-up nighttime men's club, replete with music, drinking, chatter, and a regimented protocol: you park on the inside curve of a big circular lot with numbered spots, backing your car in so you can drive directly out. At the appointed hour, a park ranger emerges with a flashlight and a wheel of those tickets they use at raffles; everybody starts his engine, and in order you roll up and receive up to four tickets, depending on how many are in your car.

I didn't know about the backing-in rule, so the fellow in the purple GTO in the next slot honked and rolled down his window and barked, "Swing it around, buddy," which I did, causing a brief but clearly distressing logjam for the cars behind me, as indicated by a not-quite supportive round of horn bursts — my rookie welcome. Since then, I've been bolt awake, wired with activity and the discomfiting presence of other people.

Consider Mr. GTO, who has fired up what looks like a major-league doobie and tuned in the classic rock station at eighty decibels, thud-thudding my windows. The deejay (like every other classic rock deejay at this hour) is spinning "Shook Me All Night Long" by AC/DC. And then there's Mr. Land Rover, who, with every last dome light on in his high-hatted vehicle, is working on a 101 acrostics book, expert edition. Don't we all need our rest to prepare for the labors of the coming day? I get out in the chilly air

ready to offer manly homilies on the virtues of dimmed lights and soft music when I see that the parking lot has been filled, and that most of the cars' occupants are not snoring away but restlessly milling around in their caps and shorts, talking golf.

There are the salty regulars, mingling with tallboy Buds and smokes — night-shift guys and retirees who've known each other for years, this their only country club, and who group up in the lead cars for the first tee times of the day so they can rip through in three hours and get back home for breakfast and a nap. There are also tourists here: a foursome of lanky young Swedes making a yearly pilgrimage, some natty-looking dudes from the Bay Area, and a father-son twosome visiting from Indiana, Mom and Sis back at the hotel in Manhattan sleeping off a sweet NYC evening of La Caravelle and *The Lion King.*

It must be that time because here comes the guy with the flashlight. Everybody gets back in the cars, and we roll out and form the conga line. When I finally park again and get called inside to the clubhouse window, I'm nearly overcome by a repeating wave of the jitters, the way I used to feel in college when I'd attempt an all-nighter and succeed only in making myself ill from too much coffee and too many Tootsie Rolls. Though there's an open spot at 6:08, I wonder if I'll be able even to hold a club, so when the lady asks again, I say the 12:36 is just fine with me, already warming with the thought of seven and a half good hours of sleep. See you later, guys. It's been real.

Postscript: Glorious day, excellent course condition, three nice fellows as partners. The one with the ugliest swing beat us silly. Suspected he was using an illegal ball, as he never let anyone mark it on the greens. I shot 83, which on any other day would have been 93. The course is long. On most of the par fours, I was hitting a three-wood for my approaches, but I was pure magic with the sixty-degree wedge, saving pars when I should have made doubles. Best eighteen-hour round of my life.

chapter 7

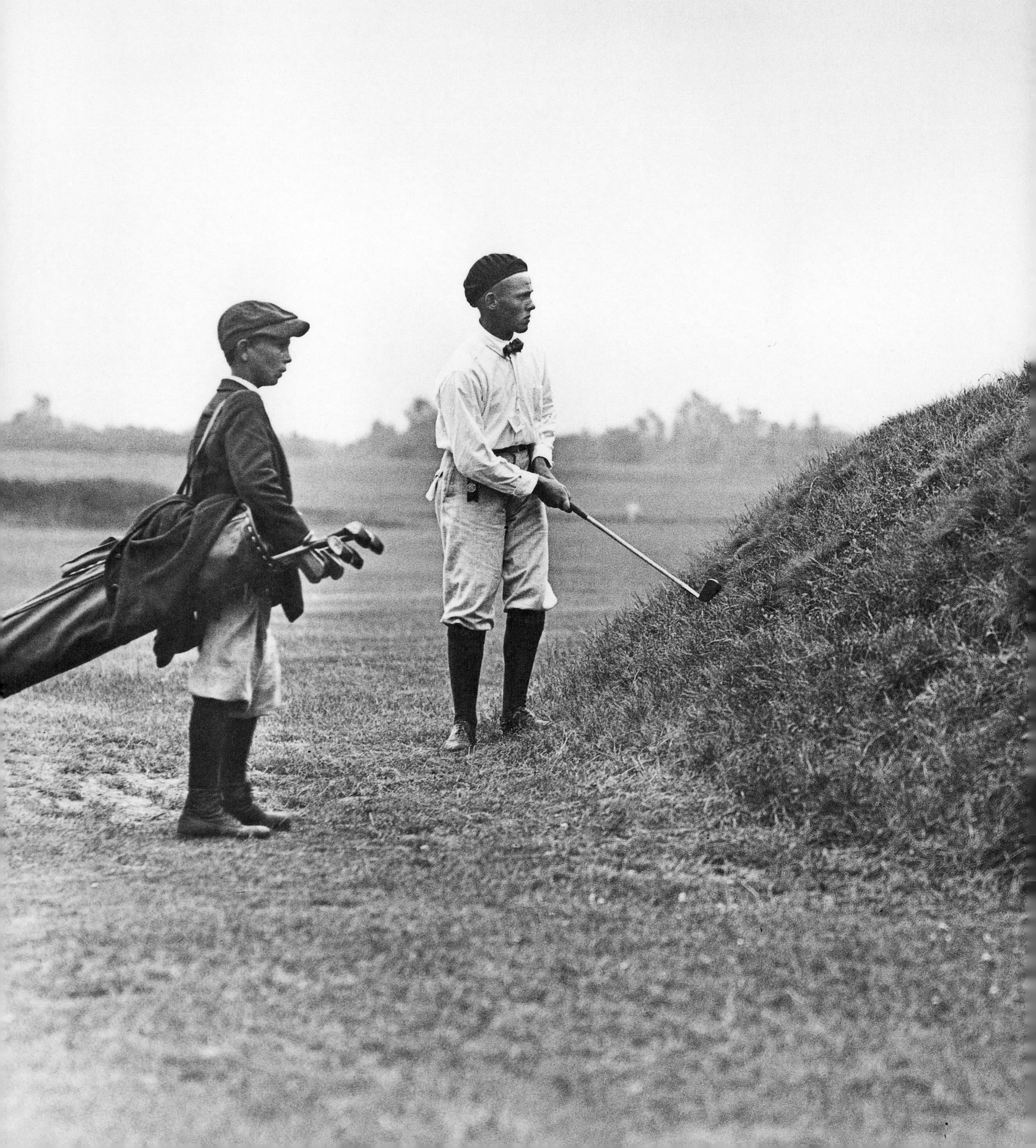

The
Course

"God is the best architect," goes the old saying, and it used to be true. In the rugged Scottish linksland, where the high dunes rolled in either direction as far as the eye could see, designing a golf course was a simple matter of looking around. Golf holes were just there, waiting to be recognized. Golfers did no more than follow the playable corridors out to some arbitrary limit, turn around, and play their way back in. At Leith and Musselburgh, the journey was short—five holes. At St. Andrews, you needed to carry a picnic hamper; the Old Course rambled a full twenty-two holes until the 1700s.

CANDY LAND: Bobby Jones, in 1901, hitting from behind a "chocolate drop" mound (facing). Above: A. W. Tillinghast mapping a course.

There were no trees on these seminal links, but the first golfers had to contend with thorny gorse, naturally eroded sandpits, and the occasional *burn,* or creek. It was not until the eighteenth century that golfers started tinkering with the linksland. They sharpened a scythe and cut the grass around the holes. They cleared little areas for tees. Another century passed, and they began to look at golf holes with a critical eye. They discovered that the game was more fun if you put the green on the other side of the burn. The sandpit was more challenging if you made it a little deeper. And since you already had the shovel out, why not dig a couple of craters where young Angus hit most of his drives? (Just to test the lad.)

The execution of these changes was usually left to a man skilled in every aspect of the game: the golf professional/greenskeeper. Allan Robertson, the St. Andrews professional, supervised the widening of the Old Course in 1848, and as part of his tinkering he put the seventeenth

green up against a cinder road and behind some mounds. He then dug a deep and horrible guarding pot bunker. The "Road Hole," as it came to be called, is still regarded as the toughest par four in the world and has been cited by golf historians as "the earliest recorded expression of golf architecture."

It soon became fashionable to hire one of these greenskeeper fellows to lay out a course. In 1851, for example, a newly formed club in Ayrshire hired Old Tom Morris to improve its crude twelve-hole links course and remain as greenskeeper. Morris stayed at Prestwick for twelve years, and he would ultimately create or upgrade some four dozen courses in the British Isles. Some were as basic as Askernish, a simple nine-hole course on an island in the Hebrides; some were as complex and enduring as Muirfield, the site of fourteen British Open Championships. It was at Muirfield that Old Tom introduced the double-loop routing of nines, each starting and ending at the clubhouse—an arrangement that tested the golfer with constantly changing wind conditions.

IN YOUR DREAMS: The eighteenth at Royal County Down in Newcastle, Northern Ireland, which was laid out in 1889 by Old Tom Morris and then buffed up later by Harry Vardon. The site, Bernard Darwin said, "offered the kind of golf that people play in their most ecstatic dreams."

The ninth at the Turnberry
Golf Club (Ailsa), Scotland.

Old-time course designers were flexible. At the Kinghorn Golf Club, a nine-holer that Morris built on the Firth of Forth, the green at the third hole, called "Loup Ower," was protected by an old stone wall. At Cupar, a small town a few miles from St. Andrews, the holes worked their way sideways up a huge hill. ("Oh, it's torture," the locals say. "You wind up with one leg longer than the other.") At Girvan, a par sixty-four cutie just south of Turnberry on the Ayrshire coast, five-time British Open champion James Braid laid out eight holes on the ocean in the classic style. But then the golfer had to walk up a hill, through the village streets, down a country lane, and through a gate to play the remaining eleven holes, which were on meadowland.

God may have been the best architect, but unfortunately He didn't build enough golf courses to satisfy the demand. So mere mortals built the inland golf courses of the 1800s, and they made a mess of it. Because rainwater couldn't percolate through clay soils, the inland

courses turned to muck in winter and baked hard during drought. Farmland was too fertile for golf; *everything* grew—fescues and blue-grasses, clover, daisies, buttercups, nut grass, barley, wheat, ferns, and melons, until you couldn't find a golf ball in the fairway. Hilly land eroded. Wooded land cost too much to clear. Riverland flooded.

For golf to flourish away from the linksland, two things had to happen: a sympathetic inland environment had to be found, and a new discipline of landscape engineering had to emerge. The first requirement was satisfied around 1900 when course designers began building in the neglected heathlands of central England. These gently rolling sandhills—the desolate moors of Arthur Conan Doyle's Sherlock Holmes stories—made excellent golf courses when cleared of scrub and pine. Advances in agronomy and soil engineering enabled course architects to satisfy the second requirement. By the turn of the century, they could clear a site of trees, drain marshy areas, build ponds, raise tees and greens above grade, and plant the prepared soil with carefully selected turf grasses. In 1901 Willie Park Jr., a two-time British Open champion and second-generation course designer, applied these new techniques to a heathland site in Berkshire, near London. His course at the Sunning-dale Golf Club had elevated tees, sculpted greens, strategic bunkering, and a man-made pond guarding a green. ("I wish I could take this course home with me," Bobby Jones said after he shot a 6-under-par 66 in qualifying for the 1926 Open Championship.) Park's work at Sunningdale was modified, over time, by the club's secretary, H. S. Colt, who became a renowned architect in his own right. Colt's Swinley Forest course was the first highly regarded woodland layout, and Colt was the first architect to give his construction foremen detailed hole drawings.

In a matter of a few years, then, the golf course advanced from its evolutionary phase to an intelligent design phase. In the evolutionary phase, courses like the one at St. Andrews emerged over decades with no one individual taking credit for the final product. In the intelligent design phase, any chap with biscuit crumbs in his beard and mischief in his mind could play God—felling a tree here, installing a pot bunker there, making the game easier or more difficult as he saw fit.

The more thoughtful of these land lords understood that golf holes, to be interesting, must fall into one of three categories: penal, strategic, or heroic. The penal golf hole presents some unavoidable obstacle—say, the Barry Burn at Carnoustie—and the player has no choice but to get over it. On a penal hole, one bad shot leads to additional difficulties and sometimes to a material sacrifice, as well—a lost ball. The strategic hole, on the other hand, offers alternative routes to the green. The golfer can go around the water, skirt the bunker, or hit away from the trees. To score well, however, he has to notice that a tee shot to a certain spot provides a better angle of approach to the green, while a pitch to a specific side of the flagstick leaves an easier putt. "The essence of strategic architecture," wrote Robert Trent Jones, "is to encourage initiative and to reward the thinking golfer while penalizing the unthinking golfer." The par-five thirteenth at Augusta National, for example, dares the player to shorten the hole by drawing his tee shot around the dogleg to the edge of Rae's Creek. "A player who dares the creek on either his first or second shot may very easily encounter a six or seven on the hole," wrote Bobby Jones. "Yet the reward of successful, bold play is most enticing."

Heroic design is a compromise between the penal and the strategic in the form of a brutal choice: go for broke or eat at the children's table. The fifth hole at the Mid Ocean Club in Tucker's Town, Bermuda, presents such a challenge. Built by C. B. Macdonald in 1924, the 433-yard

MR. SAND MAN: Gary Player in the fairway bunker on the fourth hole at Royal St. George's in Sandwich, England. This was Harry Vardon's favorite course, but he was one of few who loved it. The key was accuracy of the tee. If you missed this particular bunker, you were said to have landed in the "Elysian Fields."

par four starts on a 100-foot-high tee and requires a drive over Mangrove Lake to a catawampus fairway. The strong player can shorten the hole considerably by driving across 225 yards of water to the fairway. The less confident player must poke one on a safer line, across 150 yards of danger, and forget about making birdie. "The hole, in essence, is a seductress that juggles a golfer's heart and soul by trading on greed and fear," writes George Peper, editor of *Golf* magazine. "It presents one of the great risk-reward scenarios in the world."

Not only could the best golf architects of the early twentieth century build golf courses, but they could explicate them. Alister MacKenzie, the designer for the Cypress Point Golf Club and the Augusta National Golf Club, handed down thirteen "Essential Features" of golf course design, including: "There should be little walking between the greens and tees. . . . The greens and fairways should be sufficiently undulating, but there should be no hill climbing. . . . There should be a complete absence of the annoyance and irritation caused by the necessity of searching for lost balls." Donald Ross, who settled in Pinehurst, North Carolina, and built a design and construction firm with more than three hundred employees, laid out Pinehurst No. 2 and hundreds of other courses according to three principles: "Make each hole a different problem. So arrange it that every stroke must be made with a full concentration and attention necessary to good golf. Build each hole in such a manner that it wastes none of the ground at my disposal, and takes advantage of any possibility I can see."

If certain attributes produce great golf holes, it follows that contrary attributes produce holes that are not so great. Some turn-of-the-century designers built greens that looked like after-dinner mints: uniformly square and flat. Others put their tees on timber or concrete platforms, leaving the impression that a shed had been blown off its foundation. One sorry trend was the "chocolate drop" phenomenon of the early 1900s, in which earth was shaped into symmetrical, grassy dollops, like so many cookies on a baking sheet. (To be fair, chocolate drops were

THE LAST AMEN: Facing, the thirteenth at Augusta National, the greatest short par-5 in all of golf and the one that most dramatically illustrates the risk-reward principle. Below: Alister MacKenzie, mediocre physician but golf-course genius, who also designed Cypress Point. Of all the great designers, he was easily the worst player—which is why he liked holes that to the average golfer looked harder than they were.

NATIVE SPEAKER: C. B. Mac-donald was a sore loser, but an inspired, mostly self-taught designer responsible for the National, the Greenbriar, and Bermuda's Mid Ocean Course, among others. He specialized in "transatlantic translations"—holes that echoed and refined famous European models.

often used to camouflage piles of rocks disinterred by the excavators.) Even the great Ross experimented with geometrical shaping and put rows of pyramidal mounds on Pinehurst No. 1. He later had them razed, reminding himself to "follow nature as far as possible."

For most golf courses, however, the problem was not bad design but rather no design at all. Hundreds of municipal and small-town courses were created by practitioners known, collectively and pejoratively, as "Saturday afternoon architects." These experts laid out a golf course in a few hours, marking tees and greens with stakes and leaving the client directions for construction. The most prolific of these hit-and-run designers was Tom Bendelow of A. G. Spalding & Brothers, the sporting goods company. His fee: $25 a job.

Nowadays you pay a little more. Tom Fazio, the nephew of the tour player and course designer George Fazio, got an architect's ransom in 1990 to design Shadow Creek Golf Club for the Las Vegas gaming tycoon Steve Wynn. Jack Nicklaus, as boss of his own course design firm, commanded a million-dollar fee while he was still a threat in

major championships. ("Jack is the only architect who can exceed an unlimited budget," cracked a client.) The costs of construction have risen as well. In the late 1980s, the members of Sherwood Oaks Country Club in Thousand Oaks, California, shelled out up to $100,000 per tree to have thirty mature live oaks transplanted on their site. (Total construction cost, including clubhouse: $25 million.) In land-starved Japan, reclusive tycoons paid billions of yen in the 1980s to blow the tops off mountains and fill in valleys—all to satisfy the small-ball cravings of Japanese CEOs. "Golf design today is rooted in the ideals of challenge and aesthetics as much as it ever was," says Fazio, a humble man awed by the willingness of strangers to entrust him with tens of millions of dollars. "But during the 1990s, it has been driven more and more by grand expectations."

Critics of modern golf architecture decry the trend. "One of the reasons I'm so hard on modern creations is that the power of modern construction makes it much too easy for an architect to bulldoze away all the idiosyncrasies of a property and make all his courses look too much alike," writes Tom Doak, an American course designer

and proselytizer. "Waterfalls are created nowadays in areas with neither water nor a place for it to fall." Touring professionals of the 1990s characterized the new tournament courses, with their railroad-tie bulkheads and island greens, as overly penal and not as much fun to play. "Do the architects realize how much we hate the new courses?" asks Paul Azinger, a former PGA champion.

Certain architects actually invite such criticism, confident that the whining does nothing to hurt their status with their real constituency — recreational golfers and real estate developers. "I don't hate golfers," purred Robert Trent Jones, whose stern renovation of Oakland Hills Country Club for the 1952 U.S. Open made the pros apoplectic. "I've never built a course on which a professional couldn't score 65 if he's playing well." Indiana native Pete Dye, whose penchant for lateral water hazards, bottomless bunkers, and severe slopes culminated in the Tournament Players Club of Sawgrass in Ponte Vedra Beach, Florida, argues that the fault lies with the wussy pros, not with the courses. "Poor golfers love difficult golf courses," Dye says. "The eighteen- or nineteen-handicapper can't break par, so what he's looking for is 'the shot.' He

PINE BARONS: Pine Valley under construction circa 1920. The most spectacular and challenging of American courses was the brainchild of George Crump, a Philadelphia hotel owner, who bought some New Jersey wasteland and enlisted English architect H. S. Colt, who for eight years lived on the site like a hermit.

The fifth at the Mid Ocean
Club in Bermuda.

The fifteenth at Cypress
Point, which has been
called the Sistine Chapel
of Golf.

Following pages, clock-
wise from left: Some classic Donald Ross entrap-
ments at Pinehurst No. 2;
the "Pews" on the third
at Oakmont; a Robert Trent
Jones Jr. course at Corde
Valle in southern California; and a Zen-inspired
bunker at Horin Country
Club in Ichihara, Japan.

THE MASTER BUILDERS:
Donald Ross, the Scot who became America's most prolific golf designer, with some 400 courses to his credit. The most famous of them was Pinehurst No. 2, with which Ross tinkered all his life. Facing: The eighteenth hole at Bethpage Black, a municipal course on Long Island that was one of A. W. Tillinghast's last designs and one that rigorously demonstrates both his philosophy of penal design and his flair for drama.

holes out of a trap somewhere, and he forgets about the other ninety-three shots. He made par at the Calamity, and that's the shot he goes home with."

Maybe so, but traditional course design was on the rebound by century's end, with young architects extolling and often mimicking the look of pre–World War II grand masters such as A. W. Tillinghast (Baltusrol, Winged Foot, Bethpage Black), C. B. Macdonald (Yale, Greenbriar Old White, Monterey Peninsula), Seth Raynor (the Country Club of Charleston), Perry Maxwell (Southern Hills, Prairie Dunes), George C. Thomas Jr. (Bel-Air, Riviera), and the "Toronto Terror," Stanley Thompson (Jasper Park, Banff Springs). "We always like to set a golf course down quietly in its surroundings," said the two-time Masters champion Ben Crenshaw, who partnered with the designer Bill Coore in the creation of the Sand Hills Golf Club in Nebraska, a triumph of naturalist design. Some young designers follow the old Donald Ross dictum—"design on land, not on paper"—and do most of their work in the field, driving a bulldozer or power rake. "The best result is achieved by constant tweaking," says Bobby Weed, a Pete Dye protégé and card-carrying member of the Donald Ross Society. "You can't do it on a computer."

Nor can you rush it. A golf course is ready when the experts say so, and not a decade sooner. Between 1980 and 2002, the youngest golf course chosen to host a U.S. Open Championship was twenty-nine-year-old Hazeltine National Golf Club in Chaska, Minnesota. The oldest—The Country Club in Brookline, Massachusetts—opened in 1893. Across the Atlantic, where the ancient is even more revered, the British Open is still played every few years on the Old Course at St. Andrews, the oldest course in the world. "It is the ultimate links," writes Andre-Jean Lafaurie, "a bare landscape upon which it would be impossible to imagine anything other than magic lawn, an immense strip of straight fairway."

Sounds like God's work, all right.

Supreme
Architect

BY BRADLEY S. KLEIN

Most of the golf course designers during the Golden Age of Architecture, between the two world wars, had a vivid personality. A. W. Tillinghast, Charles Blair Macdonald, and Alister MacKenzie were flamboyant, hard-living, near-egomaniacs who managed to accumulate and then squander vast personal fortunes. Such traits may have helped them create great golf courses but were not conducive to stable, long-term careers. Not so Donald J. Ross, the most modest, the most sober, and also the most productive of all the interwar course designers.

Throughout his career, Ross remained a devoted family man. His greatest vices were an afternoon scotch and a steady if modest commitment to cigars. A self-educated man, he confined his reading matter to newspapers and magazines, not books. He was not much of an analytical thinker. His posthumously published set of essays, *Golf Has Never Failed Me* (1996), most of them written in the 1910s and 1920s, details construction technique and agronomy but lacks the flair of other classic texts on course architecture. But when Ross died in 1948, he left behind a virtual empire of course designs—399 layouts in all—including such legendary championship venues as Oak Hill Country Club (New York), Oakland Hills Country Club (Michigan), Pinehurst No. 2 (North Carolina), and Seminole (Florida).

Ross was born in 1872 in the northern Scottish town of Dornoch. There he had the run of the town's famous links, where he learned not only about playing the game but also about greenskeeping and club making. A stern Presbyterian upbringing in a family of meager means taught him hard work and the moral value of reward and punishment. These lessons influenced both his personal life and his design philosophy.

He came to the United States in 1899, when he was twenty-six, and worked as golf pro and keeper of the green at Oakley Golf Club and then Essex County Club, both in the Boston area. He was also a fine golfer, with titles in three Massachusetts Opens and two North and South Opens, plus play in half a dozen U.S. Opens, and a tie for tenth at the 1910 British Open at St. Andrews among his achievements before he turned to design full-time.

Ross's big break came in 1900, when, at the behest of its owner and founder, James R. Tufts, he went to work for a fledgling resort in the North Carolina sandhills called Pinehurst. Ross's charge was to build the golf business. He succeeded magnificently, eventually designing and overseeing the construction of four courses there.

More design jobs came his way. Providence. Hartford. Chicago. St. Paul. Cedar Rapids. Denver. World War I slowed the business, but by 1919 he was back in greater demand than any other designer in golf history. He plied trains up and down the East Coast and across

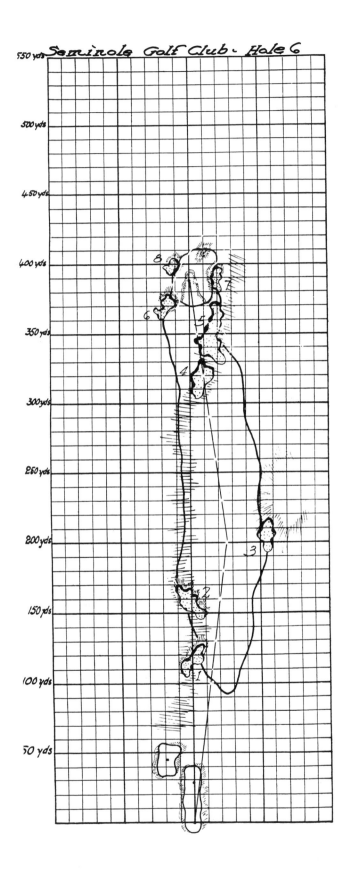

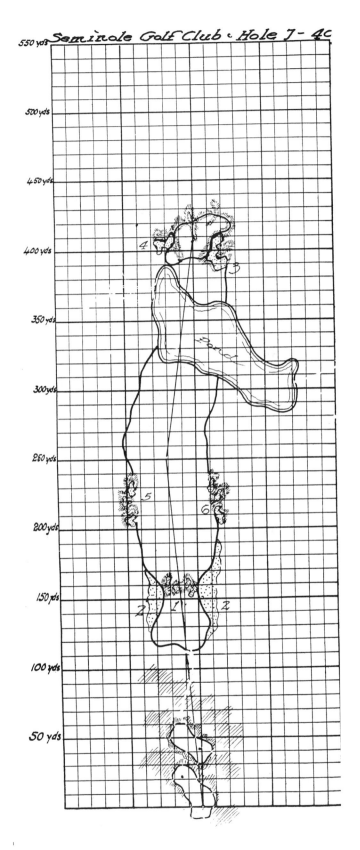

the Midwest and mid-South. Two of his design associates, Walter Hatch and J. B. McGovern, became such trusted collaborators that Ross could make do with either a single site visit or, about one-third of the time, no site visit at all. Together, he and his team completed 255 design projects during the 1920s—roughly one out of every five new courses built in this country during that decade. From 1919 to 1931, eight of thirteen U.S. Opens were held on a Ross course.

Ross was a keen businessman and marketer who promoted his club-making business as well as his design trade. Not all his business ventures were successful. His co-ownership of the Pine Crest Inn in Pinehurst proved a drain of both time and money. But he was smart enough in his design work to carry only a handful of associates on his payroll, and he managed to generate fees from both architecture and course construction. His annual net income throughout the 1920s of $50,000 to $60,000 probably made him the highest-paid person in all of golf. He was well connected, too, having played golf with U.S. presidents, secretaries of state, and captains of industry.

It has been said of Ross that his greatest professional disappointment was not getting the commission to design Augusta National Golf Club, and that he threw himself into Pinehurst No. 2 as a result. This may be true, but there's no evidence that he ever sought the job, that he was seriously considered by Augusta's cofounders, Bobby Jones and Clifford Roberts, or that he harbored resentment as a result of not landing the job. Moreover, Ross had been devoted to refining No. 2 long before the 1930s.

Ross was workmanlike, not temperamental. He would sketch from a topographic map or make extensive notes during a walk-through and entrust his civil engineer, J. Walter Johnson, to convert the instructions into full-blown construction plans. There were no government regulators standing over his shoulder and no such thing as a "wetland." If a swamp or bog posed a problem, Ross and his crew would drain and fill it. That's how Ross and his Golden Age design contemporaries were able to build courses that snuggled into

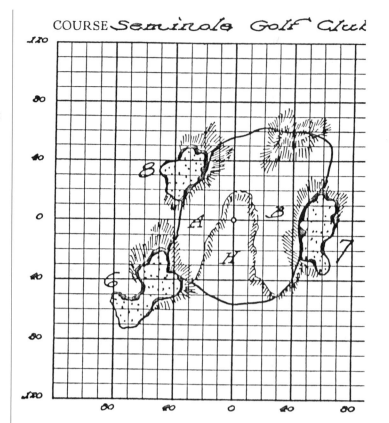

the native contours and were easy to walk, with short distances from green to next tee. Ross in particular was a master of efficient routings—the intimate sequencing of holes. He could use up all the ground on a tight parcel of 120 acres without ever forcing a hole. He had to be efficient, since earthmoving equipment in those days was limited to surface scrapers pulled by a team of horses or mules. The main skill involved in Ross's course designs was finding proper settings for each hole and utilizing natural features.

Ross was heavily influenced by the match-play ethic of his day. His elaborate design plans, for example, include the hole number and yardage but not par (for either the hole or the course). He was more concerned with interesting landforms than with scores. Ross often began his courses with a gentle par four. He reserved the upslopes for shorter par fours and would rely on downhill ground for the longer par fours. He emphasized diagonal bunkering—arraying hazards at an angle and then allowing golfers to choose how far they thought they could carry their tee shot, with the boldest shot rewarding the golfer with a better line of approach into the putting surface. Only on very short par fours would he run a hazard sheer across the front of a green. Generally, he left routes open for the ground game. In his day, courses were scarcely irrigated, and turf grass remained firm and fast. This promoted a classical links style of golf that gave golfers lots of options.

Many of the par fives Ross built were in the 460- to 490-yard range. If they play short by modern standards, they still provide gracious evidence of well-placed bunkering and swales. He never arrayed his fairways in a straight line; rather, he created S-shaped landing areas, or holes with the tee off-line from center, so that angles of play are always pronounced. Nor did he revert to symmetry or uniform curvilinear shapes. There is an irregularity, almost a randomness, to his bunker placement. And yet, because of a hazard or two on the inside of the dogleg, there are strategic options in many of his landing areas as well. "In bunkering a course," he wrote, "the aim should be to lay them out so there will be both an easy and a difficult way to each hole."

No architect consistently built more interesting putting surfaces. Many of them are squared off, so that a marginal shot on the outer rim of the green is likely to tumble off and away into a low area. The belief that Ross built domed or turtle-backed putting surfaces, however, is a myth. The tale derives from the look and feel of the greens at Pinehurst No. 2, but in fact those putting surfaces today are far more elevated and severe than they were in Ross's day. In fact, they were originally level, sand-based "browns" and were not converted to turf grass until 1935. After years of heavy sand application (or "top-dressing"), the greens acquired their now-characteristic angel-food-cake look. Nonetheless, they are uncharacteristic of Ross's work.

Ross built his greens in an era when surface slopes of 4 to 5 percent were commonplace. In his day, with turf grass on greens cut to no less than a quarter-inch, green speeds would have averaged six to seven feet on the Stimpmeter, compared to speeds today of eleven to twelve feet on greens that are regularly cut as low as one-tenth of an inch. Because of a feeling that Ross's steeply sloped greens are "out of control" at today's speeds, many course owners and managers have renovated some of their features. Many greens have been flattened, many short carry-bunkers have been removed, and holes have been lengthened to get yardage over the 7,000-yard mark. The result has often been a loss of design character.

Likewise with tree overgrowth. Ross provided wide clearings for fairways, often 50 to 60 yards across. He would tolerate trees behind tees, but not in the central line of play or on the east and south sides of holes, where leaf canopies would block sunshine from reaching turf grass and affect air circulation. But as many Ross courses have matured, they have been heavily planted over. Their tree canopies now threaten to intrude upon strategic lines of play and also to choke out turf grass.

For these reasons, a number of course architects have undertaken meticulous restoration programs designed to preserve or bring back many of Ross's original features, or to adapt them to modern agronomy and playing distances. These "restoration" efforts stand in marked contrast to the "modernization" through which so many Ross courses—and the features of courses designed by other classic designers—have been lost altogether. Among the best-preserved (or restored) Ross layouts today are Lake Sunapee (New Hampshire), Wannamoisett (Rhode Island), Wilmington Municipal (North Carolina), and Essex County Club and The Orchards (Massachusetts).

Not every course that Ross built is a great golf course; he designed too many for all of them to be museum-quality. But a surprisingly large number of Ross courses convey a gracious sensibility, are fun to walk, and still challenge strong players while remaining enjoyable to the high-handicapper. Decades after his heyday, Ross remains a powerful influence on golf.

The first at Machrihanish,
Scotland.

The Ideal Golf Hole

BY JERRY TARDE

There is nothing like the first course of a golfer's youth. You play it round and round, fifty-four holes in a day sometimes, like the second hand moving relentlessly around a clock face. You become intimate with every fairway and bunker. You even know which ball washer runs dry first.

Mine was a horrible layout that started with a par three and ended with a par three and had only nine bunkers on the whole eighteen, none with a rake. It was the kind of city-owned course where a dead body was found in the creek beside the thirteenth green once a year or so. Sunflower stalks were used for flagsticks, with empty Budweiser cans stuck to the ends. We considered them our version of the Merion baskets from the other side of town.

This course, called by the Indian name Juniata—two city blocks from my family's row house in Philadelphia, down the street from my elementary school of nuns—did have one great golf hole, the 360-yard par-four sixth. It towers in my memory as an example of sublime architecture. The tee shot was blind, and the second shot was blind, and I do believe that over the years I even had a blind putt or two. But as Pete Dye later told me: "A hole is blind only the first time you play it."

It's been years since I've played it, but I remember the conditioning of Juniata as always poor, the turf brown and the dirt under it hardscrabble. I learned early on that conditions have little to do with the greatness of a hole. In fact, overgrooming has ruined much good architecture. Years ago, I attended a meet-ing of *Golf Digest* panelists who were discussing America's 100 Greatest Holes, and two voices rose above the others in their wisdom. One belonged to the writer Charles Price, who could read a menu as if it were a papal encyclical. He said, "You should no more judge a hole by the condition of its turf than you would know the beauty of a woman by her hairdresser." The other voice in the room I can still hear was Dave Marr's. He said, "The true measure of a golf course's greatness was in the answer to a simple question: Would you tell your best friend to get off the interstate to play it?" Juniata met both tests—it was not overgroomed, and the course had to be played to be believed. In no small measure, the experience was enhanced by the cast of characters inhabiting the place, who could be described as the Bowery Boys meet the Sopranos.

Your ideal drive off number six was 50 yards to the right of center, over a stand of trees, into the middle of the fifth fairway. This caused a slight inconvenience to the golfers playing the previous hole, but I knew of none who sustained permanent injury.

The approach shot from the parallel fairway set up an oblique angle to the green. I never knew why I liked the shot so much, but I later read, as the architect A. W. Tillinghast explained, that oblique lines "permit holes to be played in numerous ways, introducing elective play and finesse that was entirely absent before."

Now here was the genius of the hole revealed. A well-struck second shot invariably bounded over the rock-hard green onto a macadam service road, from which a local rule did not allow relief. So you actually wanted to hit a low-stung wedge or a nine-iron off the second groove from the bottom of the club face. The play was to fall short and bounce straight to nestle by the Budweiser on a stick.

I still remember the anticipation time after time of running up the hill to see where the ball had finished. Was it short? Was it close? Where the hell *was* it? Did it roll onto the damned road again? It's as near as a golfer comes to the adrenaline surge a bettor feels when his horse is in a photo finish.

Maybe the hole doesn't compare to the eighth at Pebble Beach or the fifth at Pinehurst No. 2, but it was all the golf I could handle.

What makes the sixth at Juniata so ideal is not what the architects—the Army Corps of Engineers, who built it during the Depression—put in, but what they left out. The minimalism of the design lets you connect with the game in a way you cannot on a $26 million Las Vegas course with waterfalls and flower beds. First of all, there is a total absence of double negatives. You don't see a bunker behind a tree. Or worse, the popular modern convention of triple negatives: a bunker behind a tree behind a creek. On Juniata's sixth, the pure demon of the hole is the macadam over the green. It is the direct spiritual descendant of the Road Hole at St. Andrews.

As time went by and I played longer, harder holes, I would fall in love only to realize again that, as Tillinghast said, shorter holes and smaller greens are the ultimate test. "The average golfer, who cannot begin to get the prodigious lengths of the mighty ones, does like to encounter holes that are not beyond the range of two of his best efforts," Tilly once wrote. "When he is forced to face the necessity of covering 460 yards to accomplish this under normal conditions, he can't quite make it with any two shots in his bag. Yet a hole of this length and longer is plain duck soup to the great players with but few exceptions."

I learned to apply the greatness definition espoused by the five-time British Open champion, Peter Thomson. "When I first took to journalism," he once told me, "my kind but stern mentor laid down the principle that if my grandmother couldn't understand what I was writing about, it was a lousy piece of composition. I've come to carry this along into golf architecture. If my grandma can't play it, it has to be a lousy course." How can a hole be ideal if the average golfer cannot reach it? Juniata's sixth could be reached in regulation by Thomson's grandma, but it was hardly duck soup for anyone.

Golf in its purest form, at its most ideal, is in the design of a short par four. What Juniata's sixth has in spades is that elusive golf term "shot value." It poses massive risks and rewards while testing equally length, accuracy, and finesse. It is difficult while still being fair. It strikes fear in your heart—it is one of those holes you must "get past" in a round—while still being aesthetically pleasing. (All right, aesthetics in the context of urban Philadelphia.) A simple par is enough to lift the spirits, and a birdie can make the round. It fits naturally into the terrain—you are left feeling that the green grew out of the earth and there is simply no other place or shape for it to be other than where it is. Juniata's venerable sixth harkens back to the heritage of the game and, like the original Road Hole, requires you to think a little. And once you've hit a low-stung wedge to the Budweiser can, "you will glory," as Tillinghast said, "in the knowledge of having accomplished something."

chapter 8

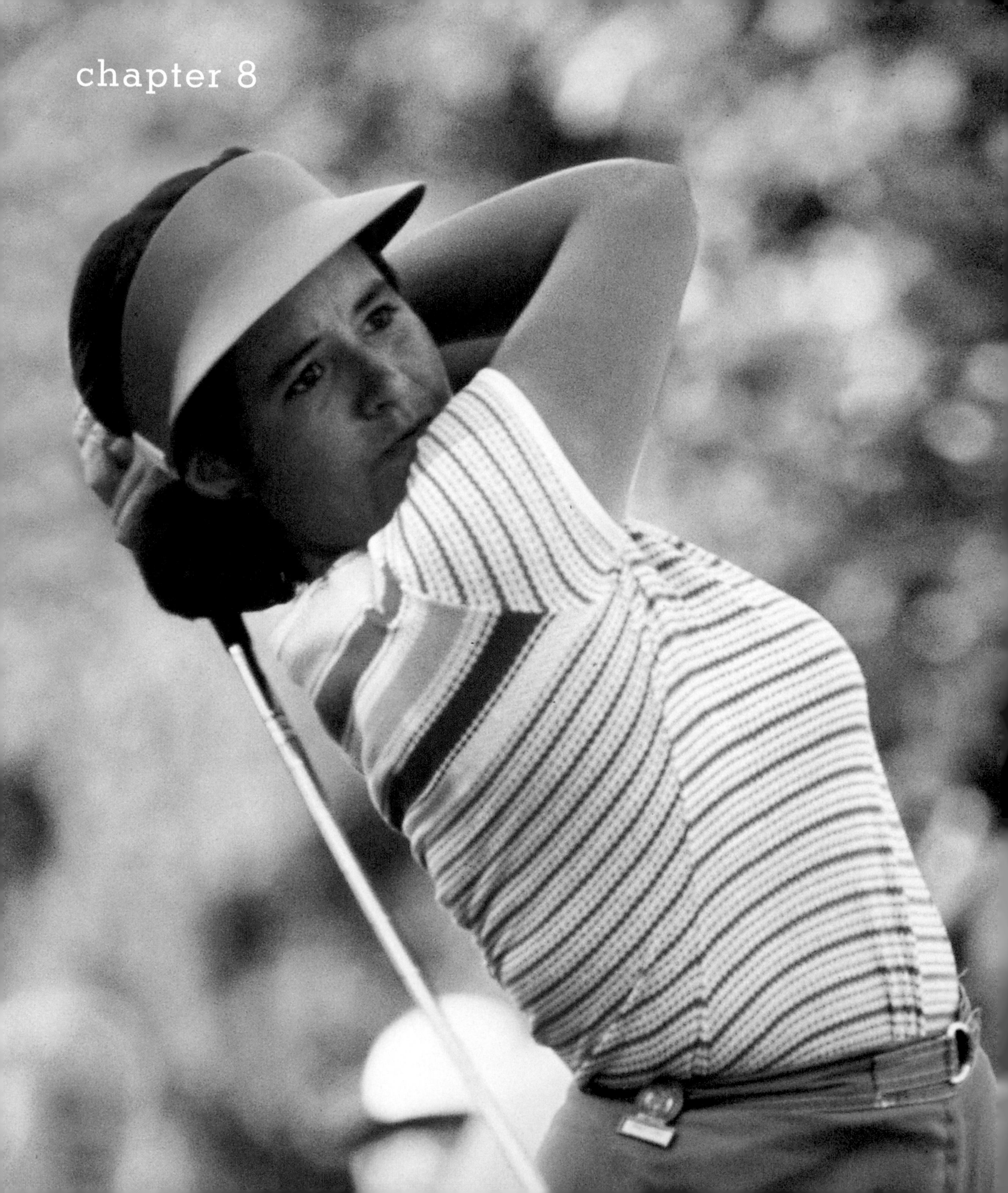

The Outsiders

The exclusionary impulse is so strong in humans that telling a complete history of practically anything requires looping back through time to pick up discarded or neglected threads. A modern military historian finally writes a chapter on the African American aviators of World War II. The new historians of the West turn their attention to the pioneer women of the American frontier. Study any subject — auto racing, the dramatic arts, the American labor movement, haute cuisine — and you find a legacy of discrimination.

GAMERS: Facing, in the 1970s, Hall of Famer Nancy Lopez consistently dominated. Above: Handicapped golfer Casey Martin needed a Supreme Court decision to use a cart in PGA events.

PIONEERS: **Althea Gibson was the first African American to play as a professional in both tennis (her dominant sport) and golf. She played with Jackie Robinson in the North-South Tournament in Miami in 1962.**

It's the same with golf, with this difference: nongolfers—even those who haven't seen *Caddyshack*—tend to blame the game itself. Mark Twain was way too kind, they say, when he described golf as "a good walk spoiled." Golf is sexist. Golf is racist. Golf is anti-Semitic, elitist, bad for the environment, and not even good exercise. "For an American of a certain age, cultural outlook, and political inclination, a love of golf is more than faintly embarrassing," writes David Owen. "Is there any sound more evocative of grody Republican smugness than the sound of golf spikes on brick?"

A careful reading of golf history provides some relief for the player whose backswing is inhibited by assumed guilt and social consciousness. Early photographs show fishermen playing on the Old Course at St. Andrews, and an observer in 1909 described working-class golfers on "a summer evening, when the hardy sons of toil, released from their strenuous lives, seek recuperation on the links on the coast side, where the land is town property." Furthermore, there have always been enough women and minorities who are passionate about the game to challenge the belief that golf belongs exclusively to white males of a certain age and income. Mary, Queen of Scots, played golf, as did Joe Louis, the African American heavyweight champ. Notah Begay Jr., a Navajo, learned the game on a municipal course in New Mexico and taught his son, Notah Begay III, who wound up on a Stanford University golf team that included an Asian American (Jerry Chang), a disabled golfer (Casey Martin), and a self-described "Cablanasian" (Tiger Woods).

The game's joys were certainly not forbidden to the women of the St. Andrews Ladies Golf Club, which had five hundred members by 1886 and held regular competitions on an elaborate putting course called "the Himalayas." Minority golfers, though rarer, were not unknown at the turn of the twentieth century. When the second U.S. Open was played at the Shinnecock Hills Golf Club in 1896, the thirty-six-man field included John Shippen, an African American caddie, and Oscar Bunn, a laborer/caddie who was also a full-blooded Shinnecock Indian. Shippen finished fifth at Shinnecock and won $10—the first prize money ever paid to an African American golfer.

Of course, golf's outsiders were often not treated with respect. Lord Wellwood, in 1890, argued for "a liberal extension of the right of golfing to women," but questioned whether they should be allowed on full-length golf courses. "If they choose to play at times when the male golfers are feeding or resting, no one can object, but at other times— must we say it?—they are in the way." When the fledgling Ladies Golf Union of England held its first championship at Royal Lytham & St. Annes in 1893, a British golf official groused that "constitutionally and physically women are unfitted for golf." He then added a prediction: "The first ladies' championship will be the last." He was wrong, of course. The upper-class women of Victorian England were turning to horseback riding, archery, tennis, and golf to express themselves. "Golf

HIT AND GIGGLE: Golf has divided men and women, but not entirely. Mixed foursomes have always been a fixture, especially on Sundays.

STIRLING FINISH: The young
Bobby Jones actually lost
a match to young Alexa
Stirling. In 1916, she
won the first of three
U.S. Women's Amateur
Championships. Like her
fabled Atlanta neighbor,
Stirling was a stylish
player known for her un-
flappable play.

gave women a sort of freedom," writes Rhonda Glenn, a golf historian. "It offered a free-swinging grace, pastoral adventure, the beauty of the sun, and the wind blowing fresh across the moors."

Freedom was relative. Lady Margaret Scott, the daughter of Lord Eldon of Gloucestershire, won the first three British Women's Open Amateur Championships in heavy, layered clothes that covered everything but her hands and face. Suffragettes and bookmakers lined the fairways at Walton Heath and Sunningdale in October 1910 when the two-time British Open champion Harold Hilton played a two-day, seventy-two-hole match against the nineteen-year-old Cumbrian sensation Cecil Leitch, the Billy Jean King of her time. Leitch could hit a golf ball farther than most men, thanks to a less restrictive wardrobe and an uninhibited swing. That she won the match, 2–1, proved little—Hilton gave her half a stroke per hole—but Leitch did play from the men's tees and shot 77 to Hilton's 75 over the last seventeen holes. Four years later, she won the first of her four national amateur championships.

In the United States, the ladies won a less-publicized battle of the sexes in 1908, when red-haired Alexa Stirling beat Bobby Jones in a six-hole match in Atlanta. (Alexa was twelve, Bobby was six, and Bobby wouldn't let her have the three-inch winner's cup. "I took it to bed with me that night," Jones recalled years later.) Stirling never beat Jones again, but she won the U.S. Women's Amateur three times between 1916 and 1920 and starred with Jones in a series of wartime exhibition matches benefiting the

Red Cross. Her example inspired Glenna Collett, who
won a record six U.S. Women's Amateur Championships
and shared the sports pages with Jones, Babe Ruth,
Red Grange, Bill Tilden, and other giants of the so-called
Golden Age of Sports. Collett's British equivalent was
Joyce Wethered, a shy Englishwoman who learned the
game on family holidays in Scotland. Wethered, in the
opinion of three-time British Open champion Henry
Cotton, hit the ball straighter than any player he had
ever seen, with the possible exception of Harry Vardon.
"Good swing?" exclaimed the Scottish pro Willie Wilson.
"My God, man! She could hit a ball 240 yards on the
fly while standing barefoot on a cake of ice." When
Wethered and Collett met in the finals of the 1929 British Women's Amateur at St. Andrews, more than ten thousand spectators followed them around the Old Course.
Wethered closed Collett out on Seventeen, the famous
Road Hole, but the gracious loser said it was "the most
glorious match of my life." Wethered retired from British
Amateur competition with four titles and only two
losses in thirty-eight matches.

Wethered's professional career was less memorable,
consisting mostly of a day job in the golf department of
a London department store and a 1935 exhibition tour
of the United States, for which she reportedly was paid
$35,000. There were few women professional golfers in
the 1930s, they had no organization, and there were not
enough "open" tournaments to constitute a circuit. The "majors" of the
time, in the United States, were the Women's Western Open (1930 to
1967) and the Titleholders Championship (1937 to 1972). Both events
were dominated by a handful of pioneer professionals, most notably
Patty Berg and Mildred "Babe" Didrikson Zaharias. Berg was the Walter

EYES ON THE PRIZE: In 1910,
British golf star Cecil
Leitch (top) took on two-
time Open champ Harold
Hilton (bottom) in an early
battle of the sexes.

FAIR WETHERED: England's Joyce Wethered, who Bobby Jones said was the best player he ever saw, was the dominant player of the 1920s. One of her rivals was Glenna Collett (seated).

Hagen of women's golf, a crowd-pleasing show-woman with preter-natural stamina and a complete game. "She knew more golf shots than any other woman before or after," said Mickey Wright, another Hall of Fame golfer. Didrikson, on the other hand, was the Paul Bunyan of women's golf, a bigger-than-life amalgam of Olympic athlete, comedienne, braggart, and folk hero. Before she took up golf, Didrikson won gold medals and set world records in the javelin and eighty-meter hurdles at the 1932 Olympic Games. She was also a three-time All-America basketball player and a softball player of such renown that she got to pitch several spring-training innings for the St. Louis Cardinals. (Asked whether there was any-thing she didn't play, she snapped, "Yes, dolls.") With coaching from Gene Sarazen, Didrikson took up golf and won eighty-two amateur and professional tournaments, including four Western Opens, three Titleholders, and three U.S. Women's Opens. She won her last U.S. Open, in 1954, by a record twelve strokes — just fifteen

ACCURACY V. POWER: Below, pioneering pros Patty Berg (left) and Babe Didrikson (right) in 1944. Berg was a supreme shot maker while Didrikson was famous for the long ball. Facing: Another power player, Louise Suggs, at the U.S. Open, of which she was the winner twice and runner-up five times.

months after undergoing surgery for cancer. In 2000, ESPN ranked Didrikson number ten on its list of the twentieth century's greatest athletes, ahead of Arnold Palmer, Ben Hogan, and Bobby Jones.

As late as 1941, the women's professional circuit consisted of four tournaments with a combined purse of $500. Things picked up a bit in 1946 when the two-year-old Women's Professional Golf Association staged the first U.S. Women's Open in Spokane, Washington. (Berg beat Betty Jameson in the match-play final.) The WPGA, unfortunately, was a weak organization. It was not until 1949, when Berg, Didrikson, and a handful of other pros convinced the former PGA tournament director Fred Corcoran to head up a new women's tour, that golf became a semi-viable career option for women. The formation of the Ladies Professional Golf Association stirred up "a national storm of indifference," Corcoran recalled years later, but the new tour did provide a stage for gifted players like Louise Suggs, Betsy Rawls, Kathy Whitworth, and the great Mickey Wright, who Ben Hogan said had the best swing he had ever seen. "There were no funds for tour staff," recalled the 1949 Titleholders champion Peggy Kirk Bell, "so we handled the day-to-day operations ourselves. One player would keep the books and write the checks, and another handled the mail. We were our own officials; sometimes we'd have to make rulings on players we were competing against."

The women pros were often the subject of ridicule—a New York sportswriter once wondered whether Babe Didrikson Zaharias "should be addressed as Miss, Mrs., Mr. or It"—but the women would not have wanted to trade circumstances with the real outsiders of American

Babe Didrikson tees off at
the 1937 Chicago Open.

golf—black players. African American pros could not even set foot on most courses unless they were caddying. Clifford Roberts, the Masters chairman, said, "As long as I'm alive, golfers will be white and caddies will be black."

The obstacles facing black golfers were numerous and arbitrary, de facto and de jure, and anything but consistent. A black professional golfer knew that he was not welcome at PGA events in the Jim Crow South, but the Los Angeles Open and the Canadian Open were, of all things, *open*. In Chicago in 1942, seven black golfers were turned away when they tried to enter the Hale America National Open, a USGA-affiliated wartime substitute for the U.S. Open. But a year later, the Chicago businessman and tournament promoter George S. May welcomed blacks to his All-America Tournament at the Tam O'Shanter Country Club, the richest tournament on the pro circuit. "These tournaments are open to any American who is willing and able to qualify," said May, staring down any objectors. Three blacks made the thirty-six-hole cut.

The ruling bodies of American golf did little to lessen the confusion. At its 1943 meeting, the Professional Golfers Association passed a bylaw restricting membership to "professional golfers of the Caucasian race"—a phrase that would haunt the organization for decades. An equally lost United States Golf Association ducked the issue by claiming that the power to exclude blacks lay in the hands of the clubs that hosted its championships. When the Miami Country Club barred black golfers from the 1952 Amateur Public Links Championship, the USGA swallowed the insult.

If discrimination deprived black golfers of the right to choose where, when, and with whom they played, it did not keep them from playing. In 1926 two black physicians from Washington, D.C., Dr. Albert Harris and Dr. George Adams, formed the United Golfers Association and began staging tournaments at a black-owned country club in Stow, Massachusetts. Before long, the UGA had its own circuit of competitions, the biggest of which was the Negro National, a summer championship played on municipal courses in the urban North. The UGA produced several players of note. Howard Wheeler, an Atlanta pro who had caddied for Bobby Jones, drove the ball 300 yards with a cross-handed grip. Wheeler got smiles by using a matchbox or a pop bottle as a tee, but he also shot numerous rounds in the low 60s and won the UGA Championship six times between 1933 and 1958. Teddy Rhodes, a sharp-dressing, smooth-swinging former caddie from Nashville, was personal pro and traveling companion to Joe Louis. In one stretch of brilliant golf, Rhodes won six consecutive tournaments, including the 1947 Joe Louis Open in Detroit. The following year, he entered the Los Angeles Open, won by Ben Hogan, and finished tied for twentieth. "I believe he was the best there ever was, and I don't just mean among the black players," wrote former UGA star Charlie Sifford in his autobiography, *Just Let Me Play.* "His only fault was that he was far too soft-spoken a person, too much a gentleman, to make waves."

As it turned out, the victories that mattered most came not on the golf course but in the courtroom. The Supreme Court's 1954 ruling in *Brown* v. *Board of Education,* which overturned the "separate but equal" doctrine

Mickey Wright, winner
of the 1961 U.S. Open
at Baltusrol

that had been applied for decades to public schools, also led to the dismantling of racial segregation at public accommodations, including municipal and daily-fee golf courses. In the spring of 1961, the PGA decided to move its 1962 championship from Los Angeles to Philadelphia because California Attorney General Stanley Mosk had advised the organization that its Caucasians-only stance, "whether on a private or public golf course, violates both the public policy and the laws of California." Boxed in, delegates of the PGA voted decisively that fall to remove the words "of the Caucasian race" from the bylaws.

It took more than a few strokes of the pen, of course, to weave blacks into the fabric of American golf. Sifford, the first PGA-approved African American touring pro, was heckled and menaced by spectators at tournaments in the South. Pete Brown, a pro from Mississippi, would become the first minority golfer to win a PGA event, the 1964 Waco Turner Open, but at the 1962 Michigan Open he had to endure shouts of "Hey, nigger!" "Like Sisyphus, blacks kept pushing the rock up the hill," writes John H. Kennedy, author of a history of African American golfers. "But, unlike that character from Greek mythology, blacks occasionally made it to the top with their rock, only to face yet another hill, and then another."

Sifford, a six-time Negro National Open champ, won the 1967 Greater Hartford Open and the 1969 Los Angeles Open. Lee Elder, a former caddie at the Pebble Beach Golf Links, represented the United States in the 1979 Ryder Cup and broke the color barrier at Augusta National when he played in the 1975 Masters. Althea Gibson, having already made history as the first

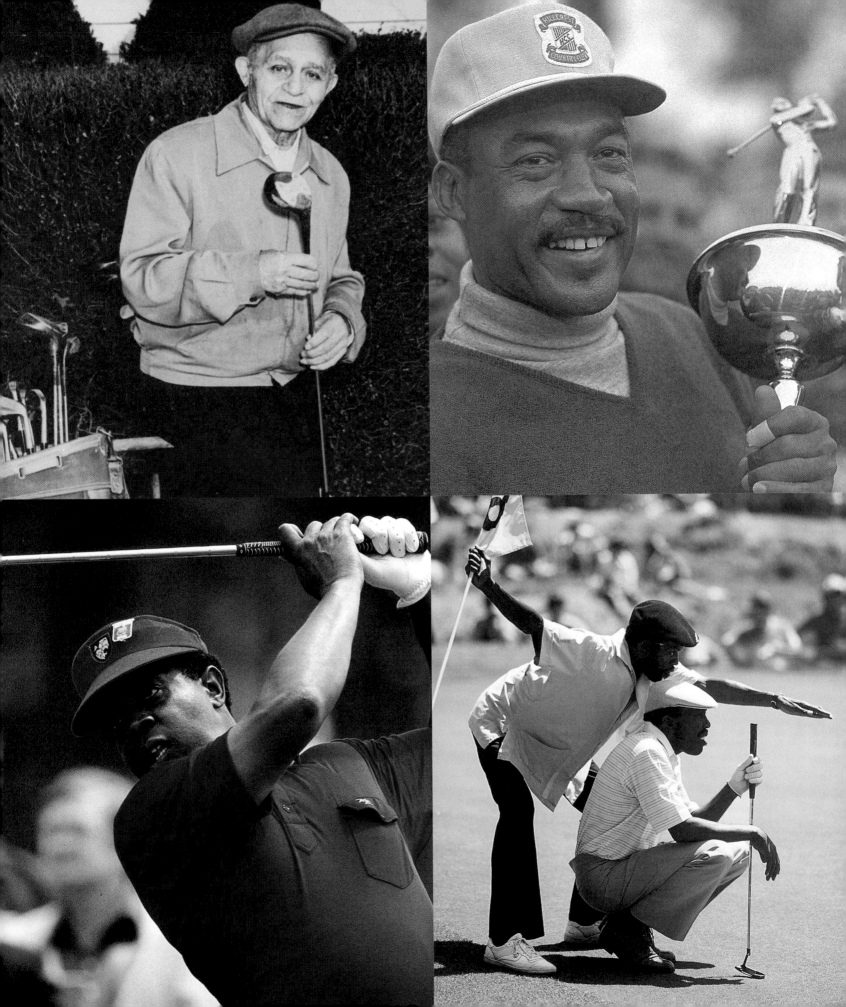

Shady Rest, one of the first all-black country clubs, was founded in 1921 in New Jersey.

African American woman to win Grand Slam titles in tennis, turned to golf and in 1964 became the first black woman on the LPGA tour. Calvin Peete, a farm salesman with a left arm permanently bent from a childhood fall, took up golf at the age of twenty-three and made PGA Tour history with eleven tour wins, two Ryder Cup appearances, and the 1984 Vardon Trophy for low scoring average.

And finally there was Tiger Woods, who dramatically and permanently demolished the notion that golf is a white man's game. Woods won the U.S. Junior three times, took the U.S. Amateur title three straight times, found success on the PGA Tour, at the age of twenty, with two wins in his first eight tournaments, and then disturbed the eternal rest of Clifford Roberts by winning the 1997 Masters by a record twelve strokes. When Woods slipped on the green jacket in the late-afternoon sunlight, his sixty-four-year-old father, Earl, said, "Green and black go well together, don't they?"

The emergence of a black man of Thai and Native American ancestry as the world's greatest player perfectly expressed golf in the 1990s, a time that found the exclusionists on the defensive. The decade opened on a sour note when Hall Thompson, founder of the Shoal Creek Country Club in Birmingham, Alabama, told a newspaper that his club would not accept blacks as members merely because it was about to host its second PGA Championship. "The country club is our home," Thompson said, "and we pick and choose who we want." Thompson quickly learned, however, that corporate sponsors and the PGA of America could also pick and choose. Facing loss of the tournament and embarrassment to Birmingham, Shoal Creek relented and admitted a black insurance executive, Louis Willie, as an honorary member with full playing privileges. In parallel actions, the three governing bodies of American golf—the PGA of America, the PGA Tour, and the USGA—declared that their competitions would henceforth be held only at clubs with open membership policies.

In 1990, the Kansas City Country Club, embarrassed when PGA

UNTOUCHABLE: From the time he was three, Tiger Woods has been a TV star. His records include three straight U.S. Amateurs (1994–96) and three consecutive U.S. Junior Amateur titles (1991–93).

Tour star Tom Watson quit over the blackballing of a prospective Jewish member, quickly reversed itself and instituted a nondiscriminatory membership policy. The Augusta National Golf Club admitted its first black member, a cable TV executive. Hundreds of other clubs, aware that women were talking to their lawyers about preferential tee times for men, sexually segregated grill rooms, and unfair treatment of divorced women and widows, changed their bylaws to conform to state and federal law. And just when the tour players thought they could tee it up without fear of a lawsuit, along came Casey Martin, an appealing young Oregonian with the power game of Phil Mickelson and the right leg of Tiny Tim. Martin sued the PGA Tour under the Americans with Disabilities Act for the right to use a motorized cart in tour events for which he was otherwise qualified to play. In 2001 the U.S. Supreme Court, in a 7–2 decision, ruled for Martin.

As a consequence of these historic changes, golf in the twenty-first century is fairer and less exclusionary than it has ever been. Most large cities now have a PGA-Tour, USGA-sponsored First Tee Program that provides playing opportunities to minority and low-income youngsters. Course superintendents are learning to conserve water, minimize the impact of herbicides and pesticides, and make the golf course a friendly habitat for eagles and silver foxes. A female golfer is now likely to inherit her husband's private club membership if he happens to drown in a water hazard.

And that's good, because it is not for golf to resolve our differences or instruct our moral development beyond the basic requirements of civility and honesty. We have churches, voting booths, and consciences for that. "Like a religion, a game seeks to codify and lighten life," John Updike writes. "Golf's ultimate moral instruction directs us to find within ourselves a pivotal center of enjoyment." At the dawn of a new century, that center of enjoyment seems within reach of almost anyone who wants to play the game.

Play Like a Man

BY HOLLY BRUBACH

The summer I was twelve, I took up golf in a mistaken attempt to spend more time with my father. Mistaken, because I had thought that golf would bring us closer together. As it turned out, my game was erratic and flashy (bogey, double bogey, birdie, triple bogey), and my father, a methodical man who ate the same thing for breakfast every morning, was horrified by my inconsistency, which he presumed to be a feminine trait—a function of that same capricious streak that prompted women to change their minds on a moment's notice or buy a new pair of shoes when they already had enough shoes at home.

My mother, too, had signed up for golf lessons, and she played with the other wives, on ladies' days. Every so often, my father would humor her by joining her for nine holes on a Saturday afternoon, after having played eighteen with his regular foursome. Playing golf with their wives, as I understood it, was the price men paid for the freedom to play with one another. Furthermore, I got the distinct impression that the game as practiced by the "ladies" was somehow second-rate. If I wanted to earn my father's respect, I would have to play like a man. To that end, he occasionally invited me to tag along with his foursome, not playing but walking the course a few paces behind, in the hope that exposure to their seriousness of purpose would somehow expunge the fluff from my game. As corrective methods go, this one eventually proved to be a failure. But inadvertently it had another effect, one

that in the end hooked me on golf even more than those occasional birdies, because it was my initiation into another world: the world of men without women.

Movies provided a window onto men in the military; novels described the life of boys in private schools. The hazing of the recruits, the raunchy humor, the blood lust—all this was precisely what we'd been led to expect whenever testosterone was given free rein. The presence of women was a mitigating influence, a force for civilization, giving rise to thank-you notes and fish knives. But the world I glimpsed on the golf course didn't conform to these notions. What set it apart from the conditions of everyday life was something far more subtle and remarkable.

At work or out to dinner, men seemed to be continually aware that there were women in their midst, and that awareness somehow altered their behavior. They grew nonchalant or they grew solicitous. They stammered or they became suddenly loquacious. They didn't know what to do with their hands or they gesticulated. Even in those instances when they went out of their way to ignore us, the sheer effort betrayed an extreme self-consciousness.

Together, however, on the golf course, they were spontaneous, relaxed, thoughtful, generous, genuinely funny, physically graceful. They were also consummate gentlemen, all by themselves. On those occasions (surely no more than a handful) when my father took me along, the men in his foursome greeted me on the first tee and then simply went about their game as if I were invisible. Which suited me fine. I silently trailed them, careful not to trigger their notice, and when every so often I tended the pin or found a ball that had burrowed into the rough, it was with all the self-effacing deference of a caddie.

Looking back on these excursions, I now recognize the thrill of watching men play golf together, oblivious of my presence, as being akin to the experience, described by nature lovers, of observing a species in its natural habitat. Men struck me as more at home on the golf course than they were in the world. They were certainly more at home on the golf course than they were in their own homes. My father tiptoed around the house, dodging knickknacks, careful not to track dirt onto the celadon-green wall-to-wall carpeting. On the golf course, though, he strode the fairways as if he owned them. Which, in a sense, he did. Meanwhile, the women trod gingerly, like trespassers, never claiming the turf, not even on those occasions when they conquered it.

If their running conversations were any indication, women regarded golf as a social game, like croquet or canasta. My mother and her friends chatted continually about upcoming parties or their children's latest accomplishments, taking time out to strike the ball every now and again. For men, however, golf was evidently more along the lines of, say, chess or baseball. No small talk. My father and his foursome, when they spoke, did so in a kind of rapid-fire, telegraphic banter: they teased one another good-naturedly; they improvised nicknames. The subject was always golf. Sometimes they called out commands to the ball, which the ball routinely ignored.

I watched and listened and learned a lot about men, if not about golf. I learned that their conversation was almost always impersonal, revolving around something other than themselves—in this case, the game at hand. I learned that they were surprisingly affectionate with one another, but that they expressed that affection through wisecracks and teasing. I learned that, contrary to what most women believed, men did not discuss women. I also learned that they were open books, if only you knew how to read them. On the golf course, I learned to read their swings.

My father's was, appropriately enough, unspectacular, slow, and steady, so grooved as to appear almost mechanical; he never took more than two putts. My uncle's, by comparison, was abbreviated, staccato (his backswing had been cut short by arthritis in his shoulder), descending to a quick jab at the ball and a stinging sound at impact—the manifestation of a personality that was nervous, quick, and debonair. I came to think of golf as an expression of something deep within, some vital energy, coiled and released in a way unique to each individual. Watching men swing, I discovered a poetry in them I might never have detected otherwise.

In time, as I got older and interested in boys, I developed a crush on a guy at the club. I was fifteen, heading into my junior year of high school; he had just graduated and would soon be off to college—a New England Ivy League school where, according to rumor, he would be playing on the golf team. That he didn't know I existed was deplorable but in the end not inconvenient, in that it enabled me to watch him, unob-

served, on the driving range as he worked his way through every club in his bag, refining his swing in preparation for the illustrious future that lay just up ahead. As the summer sun sank into the hills, I lined up my own shots and, head down, staring at the ground, studied his lengthening shadow. To this day I carry with me the memory of his swing: its fluid power—the way his knees led into the ball, the stretch into a high arc at the finish—had awakened in me something I couldn't yet begin to fathom.

Eventually, I, too, went off to college, where I, too, remarkably, landed a position on the golf team, though my commitment to the game was by this time highly conflicted. Golf seemed to me complicitous in, if not actually responsible for, the relegation of women to the rank of second-class citizens (this was the seventies). I resented the inconvenient locations of the ladies' locker rooms; I railed against the starting times (women

after 1:00 P.M.); I hated the reek of cigars that escaped from the door of the Nineteenth Hole, which was off-limits to women. Golf was one of the dead white males' many mechanisms of oppression, and I was determined to overthrow it from within. Once, as a teenager, I had won seventy-five cents from the boys chipping for quarters on the practice green, and the women's club champion gave me a piece of advice I never forgot: "It's okay to beat them," she said, "but you must never outdrive them." For several years in my twenties, I set out both to beat men *and* to outdrive them.

And then I quit. I was twenty-six, and after turning in a particularly disastrous performance in the annual father-daughter tournament, an alternate-shot event, I resolved never to play again. Fast-forward fourteen years. At the urging of a friend, I ventured back out onto the driving range and, at the urging of the local pro, back out onto the course. Now I was playing with men who, like my father and my uncle, had left their wives at home, and I was aware that for them I occupied some undefined territory: not a woman, exactly, like the ones they had married or the babes they saw on TV, but not a man, either—certainly not one of them. Still, they relaxed in my presence, despite the occasional joke about my three-yard advantage from the ladies' tees or accusations of "swinging like a girl"—leveled at one another though never at me, out of some well-intentioned if not very well-thought-out attempt to uphold the laws of political correctness. Every so often I caught a glimpse of what I'd seen when I was young: an artlessness, an elegance that rarely, if ever, got called into play at the office or on a date. If golf retains a glamour for me, and it undoubtedly does, it lies somewhere in this insight into what I've come to think of as men's true nature: their closely guarded ease with one another, which they recklessly neglected to conceal from a twelve-year-old girl. If their secret was safe with me for the time being, it was only because I was waiting to grow up—not to appreciate what I saw, which I did even then, but to articulate it.

The Jew Club

BY MARK SINGER

One of my father's best friends, a physician named Murray, a dapper twelve-handicapper in his prime, used to say that when his time came he wanted to be buried 250 yards off the tee in the center of the ninth fairway at Meadowbrook Country Club, in Tulsa, Oklahoma. Why? "Because I've never been there before."

When I heard about this ambition, at some point during adolescence, it burrowed into my imagination more profoundly than the usual bon mots of Dad's sidekicks. (As a rule, these were pragmatic men. For instance, Lester, the meatpacking mogul, once said of a par four that even on a windless day played like a legitimate par five, "I'd like to buy material from the guy who measured this hole.") Across the years, I've thought often of Murray's death wish (of sorts), admiring its metaphorical and metaphysical richness. The ninth hole at Meadowbrook was a middling par four with a cleverly placed fairway bunker about 200 yards out and, beyond that, as it faintly doglegged right, a copse of ball-eating oaks and hemlocks. Clearly, Murray believed in the possibility of immortal grace: a final resting spot from which one might launch a precisely calibrated wedge shot that would arc through the silver twilight and then bounce through the portal of eternal bliss. Murray knew all along, I assume, that in the end his wife and children—never mind the greens committee at Meadowbrook—would fail to take seriously his request. Indeed, his earthly remains wound up in the regular cemetery, almost fifteen miles from the golf course.

As an occasional consumer of what I've come to think of as the Menendez Brothers School of Memoir Writing—the literary subgenre in which a self-exculpatory author justifies his vile behavior as an inevitable consequence of a lifetime's worth of unreasonably early curfews and pitiless credit card spending limits—I've pondered how I might render an uplifting variation on the theme. Such a narrative would trace the unfolding miracle of how, despite the hardships I confronted while growing up in Oklahoma during the fifties and sixties, I managed not to become a habitual felon. Exhibit A: the reason Murray wanted to be buried beneath the ninth fairway rather than the eighteenth

since become housing developments and shopping centers. Typically, we arrived as the last bit of dew was evaporating from the fairways and the asphalt surface of the parking lot was beginning to soften. We laced up our spikes in the men's locker room, retrieved our golf bags from their cubby holes in the back of the pro shop (a flat-roofed brick structure that also included a bungalow where the club pro lived with his family), banged a bucket or two on the practice range, then pitched and putted until the coast was clear on the first tee.

By the age of nine or ten, I was playing Meadowbrook not only in the daylight but in my sleep, and forty years later I occasionally still do. Implausible juxtapositions—the stuff that golf, dreams, and certainly golf dreams are made of: the birdie sandwiched between triple bogeys, the surreal segue from the poison-ivy-and-snake-infested ravine (the price of a duck-hooked tee shot on number seven) to the pendulously ripe mulberry tree (overhanging the tee on number eight, a par three where I once witnessed my father make a hole-in-one). Not only do I see it all again in my unconscious, I smell it and hear it: the spicy perfume of fresh-cut Bermuda grass, the funk of a stagnant water hazard, the looping background harmonies of meadowlarks and whippoorwills and cicadas. Always in these reveries, the fairways and putting surfaces are lush and true—the Meadowbrook greenskeeper was a bona fide artist—and always I am a short skinny kid with a fatally unreliable short game.

In August, the club pro, Jack, and his wife, Faye, would loosely chaperone eight or ten of us on a pilgrimage to the state junior tournament. (Only now does it occur to me that this was one of Jack's duties rather than a voluntary gesture of self-sacrifice.) We'd check into a cinderblock motel, Jack would see to it that we got dinner, and then, as night fell, he would disappear and we would get busy testing our dad-emulation

was because, until the late sixties—even now I shudder at the memory of this privation— Meadowbrook had only nine holes! Plus, from May through September the heat was beastly. Plus, we were Jews.

During those endless sun-fried summers, my fellow country club urchins and I made what we could of our cultural disadvantages. Weekdays (except Mondays, when the course was closed) our station wagon–driving moms delivered us early to the club, which in those days was, relatively speaking, far out in the country, beyond cornfields and cattle pastures that have aptitudes: playing poker and gin rummy for real dollars, smoking menthol cigarettes and rum-soaked cigars, disparaging one another's incipient manhood. Come morning, Jack and Faye would deliver us to our competitive encounters with boys who'd actually slept the previous night, with predictable results.

Among us there was one genuine prodigy—Jay Friedman, who won the club junior championship at the age of twelve, defeating Bernard Robinowitz, who was seventeen. Eight years later, he won the first of two consecutive Oklahoma men's amateur championships, bolstering our faith in him as a homegrown Great Jewish Hope, our Sandy Koufax of the links. But there he peaked, in his early twenties, and his attempts to qualify for a PGA touring card always came up a little bit short. When I paid him a visit a while back at the suburban Philadelphia club where he'd spent almost twenty years as the resident pro, he obligingly and concisely answered the following impertinent question: So, what happened? "I hit a lot of golf balls," he said. "It's not that I didn't practice or work at the game. It's just that I wasn't mentally prepared. I didn't pursue it the way I should have. When I was twenty-two or twenty-three years old, I wanted to go to bars, meet women, have a good time."

Much as I admired his candor, I'd been hoping for a theory of causation that would have linked his thwarted ambitions to Meadowbrook's lack of a back nine. Because, in my own warped Menendez-like way, I'd spent decades nurturing a cultural-anthropological hypothesis of why my short game stank.

The local lore of the Semites of northeastern

216   THE ULTIMATE GOLF BOOK

Oklahoma included one anecdote that many of my elders found so unamusing they pretended it had never happened. In the early fifties, it seems, some affluent Tulsa Jews, most of them oilmen, formed a corporation whose main asset was a tract of land more than sufficient to accommodate a golf course. In the planning stages, a meeting was convened during which prospective members discussed, among other things, what to name the club. One woman, a small-town shiksa who'd married into the tribe, said, "Well, I think y'all oughta call it the Jew Club." Jaws dropped, but she kept at it: "Might as well, 'cause that's what ever'body else is gonna call it."

This was, of course, both brashly tactless and dead-on accurate. The half-dozen or so country clubs in town didn't just happen not to have any Jewish members. Some, like Southern Hills, the site of many U.S. Opens and PGA Championships, operated under bylaws or restrictive covenants that explicitly set forth the policy. My father, a practical man, believed that as a practical matter the town was run from the locker room of Southern Hills. It was this sort of provincialism that helped shape my intuition, early on, that I would live my adult life elsewhere. Until then, there was the Jew Club—Meadowbrook, our green ghetto—whose prudent founders decided not to risk the expense of maintaining more than nine holes. And so, to squeeze in a full round of eighteen one had to make the circuit twice, which naturally meant that the course was perpetually crowded, which meant that whenever I got near the green I was burdened by the knowledge that the foursome behind me was impatiently waiting, which made me anxious—which is why I was forever fluffing chip shots and hurrying putts . . .

I suppose a panel of experts might not find this terribly persuasive, either as sociology or psychology. Nor, come to think of it, did the Menendez brothers make an especially positive impression upon their jury. Finally, in the midsixties, a couple of years before I graduated from high school and moved away forever, the Meadowbrook board of directors committed to building another nine holes. This was predicated upon a substantial increase in membership—a goal that could be achieved, out there in the mid-American diaspora, only by embracing our brethren of other creeds. Soon there were Gentiles everywhere—in the locker rooms, on the putting green, in the woods. One of the first to join was Oral Roberts, the evangelist, whose trademark slogan "Expect a Miracle" made no sense to a bunch of congenitally skeptical Jews. But no matter, he was an affable fellow with a single-digit handicap.

About a decade after Meadowbrook desegregated itself, the Southern Hills crowd—no doubt motivated by altruistic impulses rather than, say, a cynical desire to remain on good terms with the United States Golf Association—invited a few Jews to join, among them my father. If you looked at the world through his lens, this was a measure of social progress. When I expressed my disapproval, he didn't equivocate. "It's the best golf course in town," he said, and that was that. He maintained a token membership at Meadowbrook for a couple more years—until, convinced that it had ceased being the Jew Club, he no longer felt obligated.

It's been twenty-five years, at least, since I last swung a club at Meadowbrook, and though I'm told that the order of holes has been reconfigured, I've continued to play the old front nine in my dreams. I found my way there one night not long ago in a foursome that included my closest childhood friend, Jeffrey Brown, my father, and his pal Murray. On the ninth hole, I hit a solid drive down the middle, easily clearing the fairway bunker and continuing on an improbably low trajectory through the open window of a maintenance worker's pickup truck. Because the passenger door was open, the ball exited and came to rest 40 yards shy of the green. Nobody said anything, but Murray nodded approvingly as I prepared to lay up with my mallet-head putter. For some reason, I'd played the entire round with that single club. We finished and headed for the first tee, ready for another nine. If I read the scorecard correctly in those gauzy hours before dawn, I'd made the turn seven over par. As usual, I felt that I should have scored better. But—as usual—I wasn't putting very well.

chapter 9

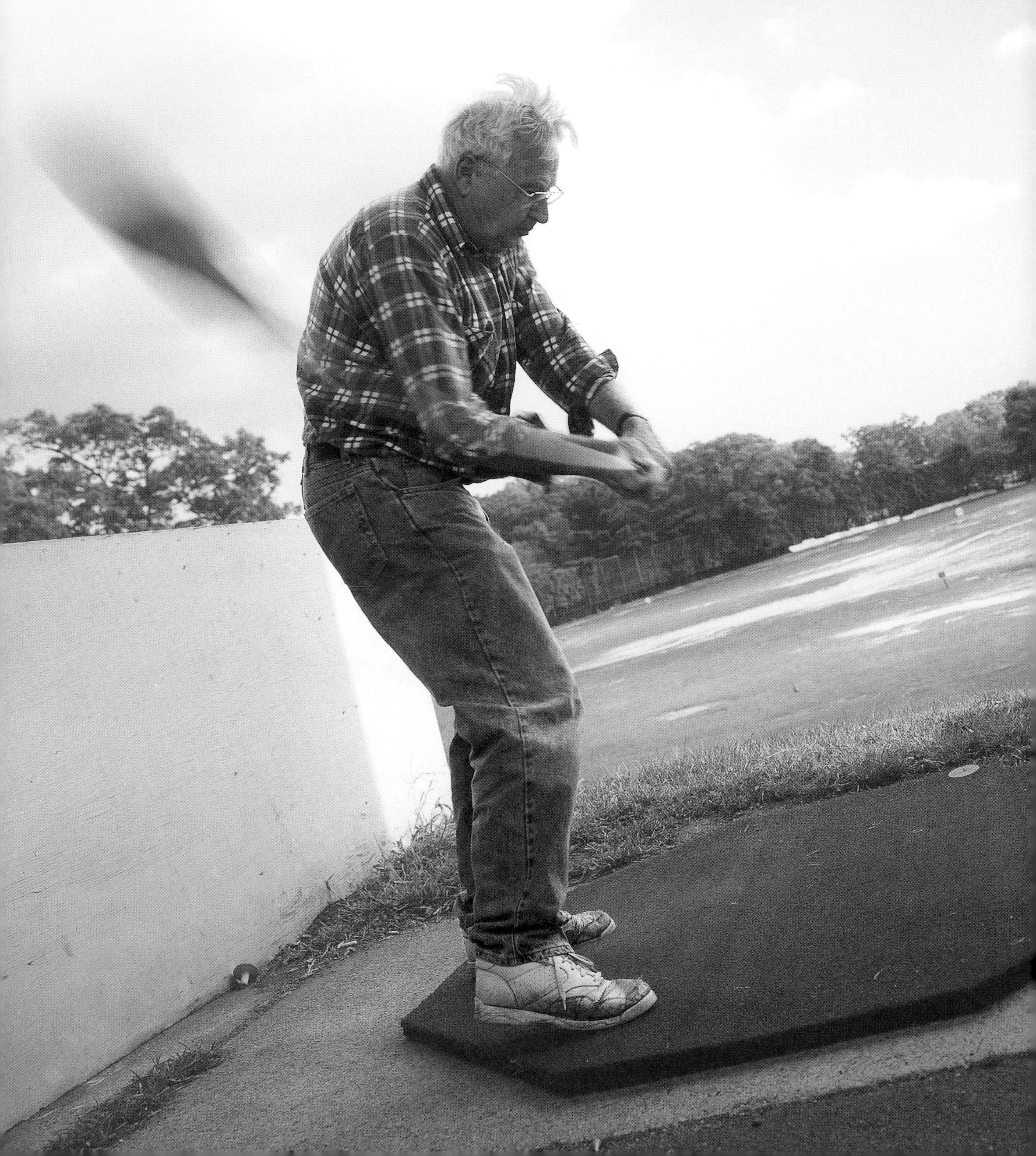

The Swing

Jim Murray of the *Los Angeles Times* described the swing of the 1973 British Open champion Tom Weiskopf as "part velvet, part silk, like a royal robe, so sweet you could pour it over ice cream." Hugh McIlvanney, after watching Jack Nicklaus play in his prime, wrote: "Backswing at the measured pace of a drawbridge being raised. Hint of a pause. All hell breaks out. Earth shakes. Women swoon. Ball departs like a shell to distant places, usually those marked by a flag." More recently, a student of the game looked at Tiger Woods's

GRIP IT AND RIP IT: Facing, working out the kinks at the local range. Above: Byron Nelson's "soft hands" were a key component to his superior shot making.

INNOVATION: Harry Vardon and the eponymous grip. He also introduced a new swing, which was more upright than the wide and sweeping one favored by golfers at the turn of the century.

smooth, powerful swing and wrote: "T 27/9, Y Fac 58°, Dr 125 mph, la 11° @ 2750 rpm, ss 375 rpm, aa +1.5, sw pth 4° ins, face 1° sh." Granted, the colleges are graduating more engineers than poets, but as Buffalo Springfield sang in the sixties, "There's something happening here."

Consider a related phenomenon: a thirteen-year-old from Thailand, Aree Song Wongluekiet, finished tenth at the 2000 Nabisco Championship, one of the major championships of women's golf. Her twin sister, Naree, won the 2001 Kosaido Thai Ladies Open. Shortly thereafter, a twelve-year-old from Florida, Morgan Pressel, qualified for the U.S. Women's Open. On the men's side, a seventeen-year-old Hampshire lad, Justin Rose, finished third at the 1999 British Open. A month later, nineteen-year-old Sergio Garcia of Spain, bounding down the eighteenth fairway like a gazelle, finished second to Woods at the PGA Championship. Aaron Baddeley, eighteen, won the 2000 Australian Open, beating a field that included Greg Norman and several

Presidents Cup players. In February 2001, Adam Scott, a twenty-year-old Australian with the build, swing, and mannerisms of Woods, won the Alfred Dunhill Championship in Europe. A few months later, a Florida ninth-grader, Ty Tryon, became the youngest player to qualify for a PGA Tour event, finishing twenty-eighth at the Honda Classic.

The performances of these precocious squirts were not fortuitous. Just as the thirteen-year, $500 million Human Genome Project marked the new millennium with its landmark mapping of human DNA, certain golf scientists are well on their way toward breaking the genetic code of golf. In Leawood, Kansas, an insurance broker studies digitized videos of golf swings, painstakingly counting frames to uncover golf's Rosetta stone—"the tempo secrets of the touring pros." In Texas, a former NASA engineer measures the directional error caused by dimple-edge contact on putts as a function of putt length and percentage of compression of the cover dimple diameter. His conclusion: "Dimple-edge contact can cause perfectly stroked putts to miss the hole only on short or downhill putts on fast greens." In Carlsbad, California, an old pro with a bad toupee swings in front of a launch monitor and discovers that he can gain twenty or thirty yards off the tee by using a more lofted driver and a low-spin, solid-core golf ball.

The implication is obvious. The golf swing, long a riddle, can now be quantified, digitized, analyzed, understood, *taught*.

BOBBY GOES TO HOLLYWOOD: In his 1931 golf-lesson movie *How to Break 90*, Bobby Jones offers timeless advice: "Starting the downswing by moving the hips first is part of the movement of every first-class golfer. It is the determining factor in my game."

These days the best golf minds busily deconstruct the sacred texts: "Nobody ever swung a golf club too slowly," said the great Bobby Jones. ("Players who hit the ball a long way are swinging *fast*," responds the Texas teaching pro Hank Haney.) "The swing plane is parallel to an imaginary pane of glass," said the great Ben Hogan. ("Other players trying to copy [Hogan's] move would probably get tied up in knots," writes the famous swing coach David Leadbetter.) "Pause briefly at the top of the backswing," said the great Tommy Armour. ("A ruinous move and something Armour didn't do himself," says the well-read pro at your local driving range.)

If the message seems to be that the great players of the past didn't know what they were doing . . . well, yes, that is the message. Jones thought he was swinging slowly. Hogan thought he swung under a pane of glass. Armour thought he paused at the top. Golf is like dance: the subjective experience does not always conform to reality. For that reason, the golfer has always been the most vulnerable of sportsmen, racked with doubt and hobbled by vague apprehensions. "Golf gives you plenty of time to worry between shots," observed the American parodist Ring Lardner. "That is the principal difference between golf and fencing."

The earliest golfers, it is said, had

a great advantage: no teachers. In fact, they had the best teacher of all: the golf ball. The flight of the ball informed their swings—high, low, left, right, short, long. They gripped their wooden baffing spoons with the hands slightly separated. They addressed the ball with their backs rounded and the forward foot pulled well back from the target line. They swung the club back on an inside path. "On the downswing you had to make an effort to roll the right hand and arm over the left to get the club face back to square at impact," says the two-time Masters champion Ben Crenshaw, a swing scholar. "Old Tom Morris and Young Tom Morris, Harry Vardon, Walter Hagen, Jones, and other greats of

the hickory shaft era didn't swing this way because they didn't know better—the shaft forced them to swing this way."

The swing gained sophistication in the late nineteenth century, when the better players discovered that they gained power and control by gripping the club in the fingers more than in the palms. Johnny Laidlay won the British Amateur in 1889 and 1891 with such a grip, unifying his hands by putting the pinky of his right hand in the channel between the knuckles of his left index and middle fingers. This overlapping grip became known as the "Vardon grip" when the English champion used it to win six Open championships. Vardon, however, did not

MOMENT OF TRUTH: A square clubface at impact is what counts, and the Trevino herky-jerk (top) and the Furyk loop de loop (bottom) prove it doesn't matter how you get there.

exploit his technical knowledge by writing an instruction book. "It all sounds so obvious when put on paper," he told the English golfer Henry Cotton, "that I always felt that anyone who did not know that much about golf should not be playing it."

After Vardon, the swing template for the aspiring golfer was Bobby Jones. Jones went to Hollywood in 1931 and filmed twelve one-reel instructionals for Warner Brothers. Some years later, he analyzed his own swing in a book, *Golf Is My Game.* "As nearly as I can describe the sensation of striking a golf ball," he wrote, "it is a combination of a pull through with the left side combined with a slapping action of the right hand and forearm, the left being responsible for bringing the movement to a well-timed climax as the ball is struck."

If even the great Jones talked about his swing as if it were a cross between a train wreck and an orgasm, what was the average golfer to do but throw up his hands and seek professional help? The 1930s and 1940s saw a rush to publication by self-styled swing theorists. Percy Boomer warned his readers that "impact must be timed correctly to an infinitesimal fraction of a second." Samuel Morrison promised that "five minutes in an easy chair, mentally rehearsing the Morrison Keys, will improve your game more than weeks

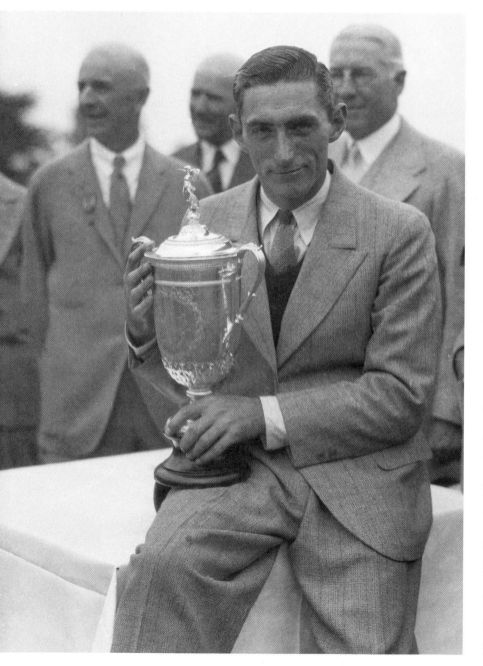

of hip-swiveling on the practice ground." The most intriguing of the swing professors was Ernest Jones, a one-legged English World War I veteran whose "swing the club head" theory and "paralysis by analysis" catchphrase sold thousands of books. Jones took a holistic approach to golf instruction. "You can't divide the swing into parts and still have a swing," he wrote. "A cat is a cat. If you dissect it you'll have blood and guts and bones all over."

At the other end of the credibility spectrum, but just as glib, was the former U.S. and British Open champion Tommy Armour, "the Silver Scot." Armour, in a pair of highly regarded instruction books, dispensed commonsense swing advice along with uncommonly sensible tips on course management. "There are two sound rules for low scoring," Armour wrote in *How to Play Your Best Golf All the Time.* "Play the shot you've got the greatest chance of playing well, and play the shot that makes the next shot easy."

When they weren't cashing royalty checks, Ernest Jones and Armour extended the parameters of the individual golf lesson. Jones taught in a dimly lit loft in a New York skyscraper, arriving most mornings in a double-breasted suit with a boutonniere. He then played Viennese waltzes on a phonograph while his pupils hit balls into a canvas curtain. Armour, willing to suffer fools only if he could do it under a beach umbrella while sipping a cocktail, set up shop on the practice tee at the Boca Raton Club, where he charged $50 for a half-hour's instruction. His standard advice: "Hit the hell out of the ball with your right hand."

The touring pros, for the most part, scoffed at mechanistic approaches to the game, claiming that their skills were the result of

MASTER CLASS: Top, two-time PGA winner (1934, 1938) and short-game specialist Paul Runyan has taught legions of golfers, including Gene Littler, Mickey Wright, and Tommy Aaron. Bottom: Butch Harmon, son of Claude and teacher of Tiger.

instinct, "feel," and other natural gifts. In this regard, they were like the jazz trumpeter Miles Davis, who mastered every scale in the Western canon while publicly asserting that his music flowed from some mystical source. "The pros then didn't talk about square-to-square and other abstrusities," writes Charles Price. "The pros didn't talk about such things because they had been too busy all day inventing them."

The two most important inventors were Byron Nelson and Ben Hogan—who, not coincidentally, were the two most dominant players of their time. Nelson, who learned to play with hickory shafts, is generally credited with developing the modern "quiet hands" swing, which works with stiff, steel-shafted clubs. His shallow divot "looked like a dollar bill," said Harvey Penick, the legendary Texas teaching pro—evidence that Nelson kept the club face square through impact longer than other players. Hogan's breakthroughs were more Einsteinian, in the sense that they appeared to express the fundamental nature of the swing while remaining incomprehensible to anyone but Hogan himself. In *Five Lessons: The Modern Fundamentals of Golf,* Hogan dazzled readers with the minutiae of pronation, supination, and his famous pane of glass. In a 1955 *Life* magazine article, he generously shared the swing "secret" that had transformed him from a hook-plagued also-ran into the greatest ball striker the game had ever known. Four decades later, deep thinkers and CIA analysts were still trying to figure out what the secret was.

Not everyone, of course, found their golf swing in a bookshop. In 1978 and 1979, Nancy Lopez won seventeen LPGA tournaments with a dazzling smile and a slow, bad-by-muny-standards backswing that had TV analysts scratching their heads. Doug Sanders, a Texas playboy who spent more time painting his shoes in carnival colors than he did prac-

Swing Theory

BYRON NELSON:
Nelson changed his swing to fit the new steel shafts. He used less hand action, put more movement in his legs, and actually dropped down through impact.

TOM WEISKOPF:
Weiskopf's swing has always been easier and more unruffled than his temper. He takes it back smoothly and keeps it back until almost the moment of impact before finishing with a big reverse C.

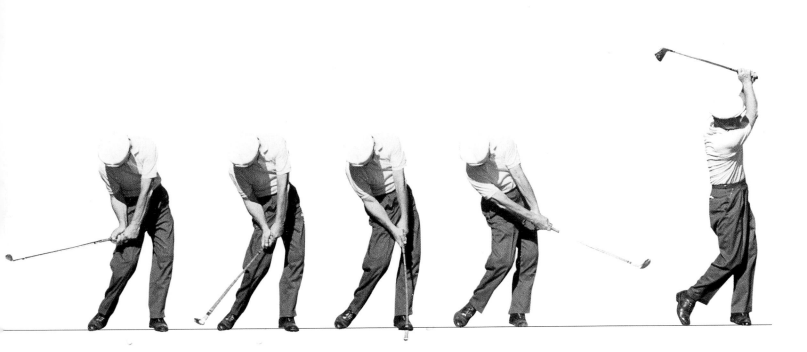

PAYNE STEWART:
The classic swing, the one that ordinary golfers dream of. Perfect balance, perfect weight shift, perfect rhythm, Stewart's swing was as efficient as it was good-looking. It was a swing built to withstand pressure.

KARRIE WEBB:
No one could ever accuse Karrie Webb of swinging like a girl. Her Tiger-like extension and big turn generate enormous torque, which she then unleashes with a powerful drop into the slot.

ticing, won twenty PGA Tour events with a backswing so short it was said he could swing inside a telephone booth. Another Texan, Lee Trevino, took the club outside on the way back and rerouted it on the way down—a tempo-killing fandango that didn't keep him from winning two U.S. Opens, two British Opens, and two PGA Championships. The worst swing of all? It belonged to the four-time Ryder Cupper Eamon Darcy of Ireland, whose jerky pass at the ball was sometimes mistaken for a grand mal seizure.

If swings like these made playing partners want to look away, other swings seduced the eye. In the 1960s, the most-copied form belonged to Gene Littler, a twenty-nine-time tour winner whose economy of motion was as simple and elegant as a Count Basie piano lick. In the 1970s, the pros admired wiry Al Geiberger, whose impeccable tempo helped him shoot a 59, the first in tour history, at the 1977 Memphis Classic. They also stood on the practice range behind the self-destructive Tom Weiskopf, winner of the 1973 British Open (and painful-to-watch runner-up in four Masters), and the brilliant but streaky Johnny Miller, whose swing thought while shooting a final-round 63 to win the 1973 U.S. Open was "Don't shank it."

Ironically, the most successful players of the period were neither those with the bad swings nor those with the good swings, but those *searching* for a swing. Tom Watson, a mop-haired scrambler from Kansas City, Missouri, took regular lessons from his club pro and flew to Texas to consult with Byron Nelson whenever his drives found the trees

too often. A tinkerer and tireless practicer, Watson won eight major championships and made an indelible impression by twice beating Jack Nicklaus at his best—at Turnberry in 1977 and Pebble Beach in 1982. "Watson scares me," Trevino said. "If he's lying 6 in the middle of the fairway, there's some kind of way he might make a 5."

Nick Faldo and Nick Price—"the two Nicks"—outdid Watson by junking their swings and starting over. Faldo, a self-involved Englishman with a Hoganesque ability to make others feel as if they were bugs on his windshield, decided in 1985 to rebuild his swing with the aid of a tall, knobby Rhodesian pro named David Leadbetter. When Faldo won the 1987 British Open with his new swing, he was launched on a decade of dominance (six major championships), and his teacher went into orbit as CEO of an international chain of golf academies. Price, a Zimbabwean air force veteran with a warm personality, started out with a loose, aggressive swing that suffered from what he called "a tense, congested position" at setup. With Leadbetter's help, Price got all his parts back in the box and won four majors plus the 1993 and 1994 PGA Tour money titles.

By the 1990s, it was unusual to see a great player without a "swing guru" at his side. Greg Norman, arguably the best player in the world from 1986 to 1995, worked with Leadbetter and with Butch Harmon, one of the four teaching-pro sons of the 1948 Masters champ Claude Harmon. Phil "Lefty" Mickelson, the best college player in a generation, took lessons from Dean Reinmuth and Rick Smith and racked up seventeen tour wins by age thirty. Davis Love III, a moneymaking machine and the 1997 PGA champion, was the *son* of a teaching pro. Technique, obviously, was a tonic. When a writer said he was looking for Leadbetter at a tournament some years ago, the PGA European Tour director Ken Schofield cracked, "I hope you find him because if you don't, about forty of our players will have nervous breakdowns."

With so many dedicated workaholics finding success on the

UP AND DOWN: Lob-meister Phil Mickelson combines fearless greenside creativity with a complete power game. It's no wonder that he still bears the burden of being labeled the "best player to have never won a major."

world's tours, it was inevitable that there would be a backlash in the recreational ranks. The weekend golfer didn't have sixty hours a week to beat balls and analyze his divots, and he sure as hell couldn't afford Leadbetter's $2,000-a-day fee (which was just Leadbetter's indirect way of saying, "Sorry, I'm busy"). Not to worry, said W. Timothy Gallwey. "Telling our bodies how to do something is not the most effective way to improve performance," Gallwey wrote in his 1979 bestseller, *The Inner Game of Golf.* "Our muscles don't understand English. . . . The secret to increasing control over our bodies lies in gaining some measure of control over our minds." The same lesson, expressed less pedantically, made a million-copy seller of *Golf in the Kingdom,* a novel by Stanford-educated Michael Murphy, cofounder of a California human potentiality factory called the Esalen Institute. "Ye try too hard and ye think too much," Murphy's Scottish golf pro tells him during a round at the fictional Burningbush. "Why don't ye go wi' your pretty swing? Let the nothingness into your shots."

With the mind-versus-mechanics debate sundering the golf world, the time was ripe for a golfer who embodied both principles. That golfer was Eldrick T. Woods. Tiger hit tennis balls with a vacuum cleaner attachment when he was still in diapers, drove golf balls into a net on national TV when he was two, and shot 48 for nine holes when he was three—all before he could have had any conscious understanding of swing mechanics. To the mystically inclined, Woods was golf's child *rinpoche.* On the other hand, the grown-up Tiger Woods immersed himself in swing theory, practiced long hours, and hired Butch Harmon as his full-time golf coach. After winning his first major, the 1997 Masters, by a tournament-record twelve strokes, Woods rebuilt his entire game, à la Faldo. Some thought the youngster was crazy—he won only one PGA Tour event in 1998 and looked like he was back-sliding—but Woods soon cut loose with the greatest stretch of play in the game's history. Between 1999 and 2001, he achieved a supernatural 50 percent PGA

Tour win rate. He won six tour events in a row. He won the Memorial Tournament three straight times. He won the 2000 U.S. Open at Pebble Beach by a major championship–record fifteen strokes. He took the British Open by eight with a major championship–record 19-under-par. When he won the Masters again in 2001, Woods held all four major titles at the same time—the so-called Tiger Slam.

Credit science. With modern optics and computer technology, Woods's perfect swing—or your imperfect swing—can be dissected like a laboratory frog. Tour players now practice with launch monitors—devices that provide an instant readout of club-head speed, launch angle, ball spin rate, and other variables. When they make too many bogeys, the pros capture their practice-range swings on laptop computers and e-mail the video to their swing coaches for instant analysis. "The golfer

IN THE MONEY: "Players win Open Championships because they play smart golf when it counts most—on tough courses in the heat of battle" —from *Smart Golf,* by three-time U.S. Open–winner Hale Irwin.

who doesn't embrace technology," says Richard Helmstetter, chief club designer for Callaway Golf, "is going to be left behind."

Or trampled. In Bradenton, Florida, students at the David Lead-better Junior Golf Academy practice every afternoon with world-class instructors. In Europe, coaches for the Swedish national team encourage pursuit of the eighteen-birdie round—what they call "54 vision." In South Korea, children who might once have stamped out plastic turkey basters in a sweatshop are out drilling on the practice range. In Australia, youngsters work with government-paid swing coaches, nutritionists, physical trainers, and sports psychologists.

Golf prophesy continues to be an underfunded discipline, but here's a prediction: the twenty-first-century player will be marked for greatness in his teens, tour-hardened at twenty, nostalgic at twenty-five, and a golfer emeritus at thirty-two. Fortunately, the game will remain a mystery to the rest of us, the many millions who approach it with the wonder, ire, befuddlement, and ecstasy of the ancient Scots who found it out there on the linksland, under the dark scudding clouds, in the sharp sea wind of Fife.

In plainer words, on a scale of one to ten, golf will still be a ten.

Scoring

BY TAD FRIEND

Any golf widow will tell you that the game can wreck a marriage. I decided to learn it to help create one. At the time, obviously, I knew nothing about either golf or marriage. This was some years back, when I was living with a woman named Andrea. The problem was that we saw her parents a lot, and it was always lousy. They talked only about their own lives, which seemed to be all society galas (Annette), ear-nose-and-throat medical conventions (Stanley), and golf (both and each and all the time).

Andrea finally suggested that I try the game, because it was something we could do together for four hours without my being reduced to seething silence. I thought golf was for geezers, but I was so desperate to find a bridge to Andrea's parents that I agreed to take a lesson with the pro at their club on Long Island. Bob was one of those guys with brilliantined hair who put a head cover on the ground, hand you a three-iron, and tell you to smack the head cover. When I scuffled it a few feet, he gave me a lazy smile and said, "See? Simple. It's a bat-and-ball game that everyone tries to make complicated. Take the bat and hit the ball."

Right. Thirty minutes later, I was ready, Bob said, to play with Andrea. Childhood lessons had left her with a love for the game and no distance control at all. So we slapped the ball around for a few days, playing sweethearts' rules: mulligans whenever you like. After growing somewhat accustomed to an old set of Stanley's clubs — a persimmon three-wood and Bob Toski blades that I kept sticking in the ground like so many trowels — I felt ready for Operation Now We See Him in a Whole New Light.

We started with Annette. When I hit a low runner off the first tee, she said, "I guess Bob's not a miracle worker." She promptly dribble-shanked it. "Take another," I said. She drilled her next drive about 130 yards. "Nice hit," I said, having learned already that the most pleasant part of golf is earning the pleasantries. That drive would be Annette's highlight reel for the day: she'd taken up the game only recently, to spend more time with her husband. But we were all painstakingly generous with compliments and gimme putts, and Andrea was beaming as we buzzed along in our little cart.

Then I tackled Mt. Stanley. A single-digit handicapper, he had a velvety swing that made mine feel like a chainsaw massacre. He and I went out off the back tees at 6:30 A.M. one hot Saturday, and I had everything working. Trees redirected my drives to the short grass; skulled wedges rolled up close; I even hit some shots intentionally. Meanwhile, Stanley was having his worst round in years. First disbelieving, he soon turned morose, then postal. We finished with identical 96s. His silence said it all: my Furykian staggers had hexed his swing. Worse, I was sleeping with his daughter.

A few weeks later we tried again as a foursome. On the first hole Stanley hit a 250-yard bomb that kicked behind a tree. I hit a drive that fluttered to the left, somewhat by design, and then boomeranged forty yards right, into the middle of the fairway. "Oh, sweet pea," Andrea said, "that's beautiful!"

"That's a banana ball," her father muttered from the cart. "A slice."

Annette said, "Give him some advice, Stanley."

"Don't slice," he said, tromping the gas.

Clearly, golf was not going to serve for me as Ping-Pong did for Nixon and the Chinese. But I kept playing anyway, sometimes with Andrea and sometimes with friends who were also just taking up the game. Soon I preferred to play with my friends, because we didn't expect much of each other. If I was having a horrible day, I was allowed to seethe. All they asked was that I play fast and settle my bets.

Golf is said to be a social game, but often it's actually a socially acceptable way to focus entirely on yourself. Within two years I had a steady fade, a reliable short game, and no girlfriend. For a while I had loved Andrea. Then I loved Andrea and golf. Finally I loved only golf.

My golfing buddies, bachelors all, used to ponder the story we'd heard about the guy who fell hard for his girlfriend because she, too, loved golf. He proposed by leaving a diamond ring at the bottom of the cup, but the engagement soon broke off in teary misunderstandings. Was it because he had made her putt out from less than a foot to find the ring in the first place? It was the kind of vignette you mull over late at night.

A few years ago, my friends Michael and Adam and I played a morning round. We usually got to our home course in the Bronx by sharing a cab from Manhattan; this day, however, Adam showed up separately with a looker named Kate. He had met her at a cocktail party the night before and been so thunderstruck that all he could stammer was that he had an early tee time, a severe flirtation bungle; Adam had just doused himself with gasoline and handed her a matchbook. But Kate had responded that (a) she loved golf; (b) she would love to play with Adam; (c) she would love to take time off from work to play; and (d) she could give us all a ride home in her boyfriend's BMW.

She proved warm and friendly as we chatted near the tee box, and then she stepped up and ripped her drive with a jaunty swing that revealed a flash of mid-riff. She strode off with her hair swinging around her shoulders. We were in awe.

"Does her boyfriend play golf?" Michael asked Adam, who was nosing his pull cart among the trees in search of his foozled drive.

"Nope."

"You're in!" Michael said. "As soon as you can outdrive her."

Adam hit his four-iron fat and uttered a small cry of rage. His ball was still well back of Kate's drive. "Does *your* boyfriend play golf?" Michael asked. Our humor was no more retarded than we ourselves were.

"You should marry her," I told Adam. And so, not long afterward, he did. He mostly golfed with Kate after that, and we missed him.

As I grew (quickly) older and (very slowly) smarter, I found myself thinking, "I need to find me a hard-swinging, BMW-driving, Myrtle Beach–loving woman." Instead, I wound up dating Amanda. Her family did own a BMW dealership, as it happened, yet our relationship began not with top-down test drives but with a cautious mutual enthusiasm for obscure Polish films. I liked her a lot, but hung back, feeling that some emotional link hadn't quite been found or forged. A trained cook who writes about food, she seemed totally immersed in the rarefied world of reduction sauces, so it startled me, a few weeks in, when she asked a number of questions about how I'd played that weekend. She actually seemed to care what I shot, and why I was pushing my long irons but pulling my wedges.

When I expressed surprise at her interest, Amanda shyly allowed that she had played a little herself. So we went to a driving range, and she turned out to have a textbook swing. Unfortunately, her weak grip and time-lapse-photography club-head speed sent every shot arcing gently to the right. The results reminded me, with a pang, of my own slice of long ago. "It's so . . . *ugly*," she said. Yep. But she was beautiful, and so was her swing, and so was her look of expectation that I would make it all come out right. "Don't worry," I said, moving her hands and feet a little to align them with my own, "we'll fix it."

Course
Management

BY JACK WELCH

There are two schools of thought about whether it's a good idea to play golf with your spouse. One is: No way! The whole point of golf is to get some time off. And the other is: Why not? You might even get to play more often. I've been married twice, and I've subscribed to both beliefs. I can say with conviction that the second way is better — though, as is so often the case with golf, I discovered it late and almost by accident. I sometimes think, in fact, that everything in golf happens backwards. You start out playing with a taped-up club and with balls you found in the woods. You don't get the good equipment until you're almost too old to appreciate it, and often it's just given to you. When you're young you have to sneak on. But when you're older and can afford to come though the gate and lucky enough to belong to a club, you're often too busy.

In 1989 I had just remarried. My new wife, Jane, was a mergers and acquisitions lawyer — an associate — and she was working day and night. Finally, after some major negotiations with her bosses, she managed to get a weekend off, and I took her to Nantucket. On Friday night we went out to dinner, and I showed her around the island. On Saturday morning I woke up, got dressed, and started to walk out the door.

"Where the hell are you going?" Jane said.

I said, "I'm going golfing."

"You're kidding," she said. "I have to practically

sign away my birthright to get this weekend and you're going golfing?"

I honestly didn't know any better. This is what I did when I was married the first time, and it's what I thought you were supposed to do. You worked hard all week, and then on Saturday morning you got dressed and went out the door to play golf with the guys.

That could have been the beginning of the end right there, but instead Jane said something that changed both of our lives. She said, "Hell, if you're going to do that, then I'm going to learn how to play golf, too."

And she did—well enough to win five club championships. Once she made up her mind to do something she stayed with it. She took some lessons with the pro, and she took some lessons, if you can call them that, with me. I don't know how much they helped her, but those lessons—just teaching her the fundamentals—made a huge difference for me.

I was pretty much a self-taught player. I picked up the game caddying at Kernwood Country Club in Salem, Massachusetts. This was my father's idea. He was a train conductor on the commuter railroad that ran from Boston to the wealthy suburbs on the North Shore. He was an affable fellow who would talk to all the big shots, and what they wanted to talk about was golf. So he got the notion that golf was what I ought to learn. I was playing hockey and football, but he kept saying that golf was a game I would have all my life—and of course he was right.

I grew up with your typical caddie's swing—short, quick, no style, wrong grip, you name it. I never practiced much, because it's just not in my nature. I'd go over to the range really meaning to work on my swing. I'd hit balls for ten minutes or so, and then I'd have to go and play. But I could always sort of hockey the ball around. I played on the high school team and as a freshman in college. When I met Jane I was a ten-handicap.

In the process of teaching Jane, though, I made myself a whole lot better. I got down to a three, and I won two club championships when I was in my mid-fifties. In my forties, before I met Jane, I'd get knocked out in the first round every time. I wasn't aware of it, but when I was teaching her what I was really doing, of course, was teaching myself. For the first time in my life I actually slowed myself down and thought about the golf swing. There I was telling her to take a longer backswing, and I realized that my own was much too short. So I worked on getting it back farther, and I also worked on learning how to finish. Before that I never finished. Now I kept saying to myself, "Freddy

Couples, Freddy Couples, Freddy Couples," because of how nicely he finishes, and it worked.

More than any one technical thing, though, what teaching someone else brought out in me was a habit of attention and awareness. I found, for example, that late in a round I wouldn't start to leak oil so badly. One day in a friendly match I actually had a lower score than Greg Norman—I had a 69, from the back tees, and he had a 70 from the tips. But the funny thing is that at the time I wasn't even thinking about the score. I was just concentrating on my swing. I think I faxed the scorecard to everyone I know, and Greg was a good sport about letting me show off.

Meanwhile, Jane kept getting better and better. She became as intense about golf as she is about everything else. And so the game became, not a bone of contention between us, but something that we shared, and we have had a wonderful life because of that. We've traveled all over together to play golf—to Ireland and to Mexico—and golf has brought us all sorts of new friends. Often just the two of us go out, and we play for the ownership of the television clicker that night. Needless to say, with the stakes so high, these are very intense matches. I give her only one or two shots a side these days, and she still wins her share. I can see the day coming when she's going to be giving me shots, because she's seventeen years younger. That's inevitable, and I can't really regret it, because we've had such a great ride along the way.

I'm also not going to go down without a fight. In the last three or four years I've been taking a lot of lessons. I'm sixty-five, and I'm at the point where I'll do anything. I'd buy elixir from some guy driving by in his car if I thought it would grow hair, and I'd do the same for ten more yards on a tee shot. The trouble is, every time I take a lesson I get worse and I'm struggling to break 80 now. Every year I go to Jerry Pittman, the pro at Seminole, and I tell him I want to change my swing. Every time he asks me how old I am this year and how old I was last year. He says, "Why don't you just face it?" But I don't want to face it—because I'm having too much fun.

Walk, Don't Ride: the
Machrie Golf Club in
Islay, Scotland.

Golf Takes a Holiday

BY LEE EISENBERG

A bag of sleek graphite clubs stands abandoned in the corner of my garage, covered in a film of dust. Next to it sulks another bag, this one holding a clattering collection of specialty woods, wedges, and putters. Four pairs of golf shoes litter the trunk of my car. Bits of dry grass still cling to the spikes, as if to the memory of a fresh, dewy morning. These once favorite things are now what's left of an endless love that ended. It fizzled with a now-forgotten putt on a late autumn afternoon three years ago. That was when golf and I called it a day. Splitsville. Kaput.

The end really began in the early 1990s, when I took the drastic step of leaving my job to look for thrills in exactly the wrong place. It was a classic Gail Sheehy moment, the time when some middle-aged guys chase after too-young women and reach for the martini shaker. My passage was wilder and crazier. It lured me not to a cheap motel but to a decrepit driving range. The place was tucked away behind a strip mall in the small southern city where I was then living. Its only distinguishing feature was a rusty pickup with HIT ME painted on the side. The ancient metal carcass doubled as the 100-yard marker. On weekdays the range attracted the usual assortment of hackers bent on redemption: sales reps who sneaked a quick bucket between calls; stiff-jointed geezers with tight, furious swings; and a huge mountain man in overalls and Pennzoil cap who came down from the Smokies, wielding a murderous driver. He was drawn by the fact that here for eight bucks you could buy an enormous bushel full of balls, otherwise known as a Big Bubba.

An impulsive notion had brought me to this ramshackle place, a stray thought that flared into a grand delusion before I could douse it. I'd become obsessed with the idea of a grand quest, a hacker's rendezvous with destiny. The plan was to put aside responsible work and family outings. Hit Big Bubbas till the cows come home. Acquire an arsenal of harnesses, braces, swing aids, and other widgets that held the promise of incremental improvement. Enroll in golf schools, perpetually. Keep a local pro on tap for weekly tune-ups. Scour books, magazines, and videos for miscellaneous counsel. Pitch perforated plastic balls, endlessly, across the front lawn. The assignment: get in touch with my inner scratch. Cultivate tempo, touch, and technique. And when the quest was over, liberate the sweet-swinging golfer I suspected dwelled inside of me, a typical twenty-handicap. Within two years, I vowed, I'd burst out of the chains of my mediocrity and break 80.

The journey played out through a dozen states and scores of golf courses, from Boca Raton to Scottsdale, from the McLean Academy to Pelz's Short Game U. There wasn't a trick in the book I didn't try. To silence negative swing thoughts, I hummed show tunes while teeing off. To ungunk aging rotators and flexors, I subjected my body to three months of arduous physical therapy. To achieve better balance, I brushed my teeth with my left hand to get it to work more productively with my overbearing right. I resorted to morning and evening Zen practice, even popped the occasional Valium, to steady my nerves before hitting the first tee.

For these two years, golf was my mistress, muse, and—dare I say it?—metaphor for life and learning. The quest offered insight into how much improvement an average grown-up might reasonably extract from inherited skills. There were the inevitable ups and downs, points along the way when progress was so stalled I'd announce to my wife that I was throwing in the towel, only to awake the next morning with refreshed hope. There were intoxicating rushes of accomplishment and revelation when, for a moment, everything clicked. I'd enter a zone and bask in the ephemeral joy that came with hitting a sweet spot.

Progress was plodding and hard-won. After repeated attempts I learned how to place my feet and set the face of the club so that I could reliably lift a ball out of a sand bunker. I learned that putts break vastly more than we give them credit for. An imagined metronome ticking in my head, I began to stroke, not stab, my putts to their happy destination.

At no point did my handicap drop like a rock. I managed to gain a stroke here, a stroke there. Whatever. I was so consumed with golf that life without the game was unimaginable. Break 80? It never happened, though I did have an occasional round when, for six, eight, or twelve holes at a stretch, I convinced myself that I was on pace.

When the quest was over, I fell back into the semi-obsessive affair with golf I'd been carrying on for twenty years. I replayed rounds before going to sleep, finagled weekend trips with buddies, kept an eye out for new equipment. I played without distinction in club events and insistently planned family vacations to places where a golf course was at hand.

Then I never played again. Three years ago and counting. That first year's leave of absence had everything to do with the fact that I'd taken a new job in a new city. The long-distance commute allowed only precious hours a week to be with my young kids. Still, for the first time in two decades I failed to carve out the time for golf. I figured the year was an aberration, that I would hook back up with mistress and muse with the ensuing spring.

But no golf sap ran the following March. Instead of heading for a course at the first opportunity that spring, I spent hours in the garden and taught my son how to fly-fish. In August we went out west on holiday, in pursuit of horse trails and trout streams. How pleasant it was not to haul along a travel bag crammed with sticks and balls.

There were occasions during that second celibate season when I'd experience a pang (a ping?) of sentimental longing. Mostly this was triggered when I'd drive past a golf course in the early evening, the most fetching time of all. Speeding by, I momentarily fretted about dopey things such as whether I'd remember where to place my feet on an uneven lie. I didn't necessarily want to play; I mostly missed the beauty and the light of being on a golf course. This longing came and went in a flash, like the feeling you get years after you let a lover slip away, not knowing at the time that she was leaving with a chunk of your heart.

Jump-cut to the present. It is now the third straight year without golf. For reasons I don't entirely understand, I stubbornly refuse to return to it. The other day some people at the office put heavy pressure on me to join an after-work league. I demurred, saying that I didn't have the time. Partly, that's true. But I'd also rather not find out how little golf there is left in me. If skills have eroded, or the fire's not there, who needs it? Or if it is, I am loath to rekindle the paralysis by analysis, the pressure of the scorecard, the intense self-absorption that flamed when I'd pick up a club. Yet in spite of all that, the mistress beckons. Last week's invitation to play prompts me to dust off a few clubs. There's a practice range just down the road. No rusty pickup or Big Bubbas this time, just a pleasant, plain-vanilla range where between shots you look up and see cows grazing on a ridge off in the distance.

Maybe it's the bucolic surroundings, or maybe it's that so little is at stake, but as I prepare to hit my first shot I am entirely relaxed. A far cry from those days of yesteryear when each swing held in its too-tight grip the imminent promise of triumph or failure. I've taken the first step back. I hum some show tunes, hit a Baby Bubba of balls, throw my clubs in the trunk, and go home to prune the roses.

Biographical Notes

MICHAEL BAMBERGER is a senior writer for *Sports Illustrated* and the author of three books and a play, including *To the Links-land* (1992).

HOLLY BRUBACH, the former style editor of the *New York Times,* has written for the *Atlantic* and *The New Yorker.* She is the author of two books, *Girlfriend: Men, Women, and Drag* (1999) and *A Dedicated Follower of Fashion* (1999). She lives in Milan and New York.

MICHAEL DiLEO, a freelance writer based in Austin, is a frequent contributor to *Texas Monthly* and has written for *Mother Jones* and *Rolling Stone.* His story "Deer Prudence" was included in *The Best American Sports Writing 2001.*

LEE EISENBERG has served as the editor in chief of *Esquire* and as a consulting editor at *Time.* He is now the executive vice president and creative director of Lands End. Among his books is *Breaking Eighty: A Journey Through the Nine Fairways of Hell* (1997).

JOHN FEINSTEIN is the author of numerous books, including *The Majors* (1999) and *A Good Walk Spoiled* (1995). He writes regularly for *Inside Sports, Golf Magazine, Tennis Magazine,* and *Basketball America.*

A staff writer at *The New Yorker,* **TAD FRIEND** has written for *Esquire* and *Outside.* He is the author of *Lost in Mongolia: Travels in Hollywood and Other Foreign Lands* (2001).

DAN JENKINS enjoyed a twenty-year tenure as chief golf writer for *Sports Illustrated.* The author of seventeen books, the most recent of which is *The Money-Whipped Steer-Job Three-Jack Give-Up Artist* (2001), Jenkins is currently a columnist for *Golf Digest.*

WARD JUST is the author of twelve novels, the most recent of which are *A Dangerous Friend* (1999), winner of the James Fenimore Cooper Prize of the Society of American Historians, and the National Book Award finalist *Echo House* (1997).

A former professor of political theory and international relations, **BRADLEY S. KLEIN** is now the architecture editor and a senior writer for *Golfweek.* He has written *Rough Meditations* (1997) and *Discovering Donald Ross: The Architect and His Golf Courses* (2001).

VERLYN KLINKENBORG is a member of the editorial board of the *New York Times* and the author of *Making Hay* (1986) and *The Last Fine Time* (1990).

CHANG-RAE LEE is the author of two novels, *A Gesture Life* (1999) and the PEN/Hemingway Award-winning *Native Speaker* (1995).

CHARLES McGRATH is the editor of the *New York Times Book Review* and contributes articles to the *New York Times Magazine.* Formerly the deputy editor of *The New Yorker,* he has also written numerous stories, book reviews, and articles for that magazine.

JOHN PAUL NEWPORT is a contributing editor for *T&L Golf.* He is the author of *The Fine Green Line* (2000) and has written for *Men's Journal, Sports Illustrated, Golf, Golf Digest, Fortune,* and numerous other magazines.

DAVID OWEN is a staff writer for *The New Yorker* and a contributing editor for *Golf Digest.* His books about golf include *My Usual Game: Adventures in Golf* (1995), *The Making of the Masters* (1999), and *The Chosen One* (2001).

A senior writer for *Sports Illustrated,* **RICK REILLY** has been voted National Sportswriter of the Year six times. His most recent book is a collection of his columns, *The Life of Reilly* (2000).

CURT SAMPSON, a former golf professional, is the author of numerous books, including *The Masters* and *Hogan*. He has written for *Sports Illustrated, Golf Magazine,* and *Playboy,* among other publications.

JERRY TARDE, formerly senior vice president and editorial director of the New York Times Company Magazine Group, is now the chairman and editorial director of the Golf Digest Companies. He has been editor in chief of *Golf Digest* since 1984.

JOHN UPDIKE is one of the nation's most honored authors. After graduating from Harvard, he joined the staff of *The New Yorker* in 1955. Since 1957 he has lived in Massachusetts. Two of his novels, *Rabbit Is Rich* (1981) and *Rabbit at Rest* (1990), won the Pulitzer Prize for fiction. Most recently he has written *Gertrude and Claudius* (2000), a novel; *Licks of Love* (2000), short stories; and *Americana and Other Poems* (2001).

JACK WELCH acted as chairman of General Electric Company for twenty years until his retirement in 2001. He has also written a memoir, *Jack: Straight from the Gut* (2001).

Acknowledgments

Thanks are due, first of all, to the writers who so graciously agreed to be part of this project and put themselves in the hands of a pair of editors who were sometimes maddeningly unclear about what they wanted. Dan Okrent, pioneer of the ultimate sports book, got the ball rolling and kept it on track sometimes with body English, sometimes with a little nudge. Susan Canavan, editor at Houghton Mifflin, did the same. Cynthia Buck and Alison Kerr Miller proved to be gracious, eagle-eyed copy editors. This book was designed by Elizabeth Johnsboen and Wendy Palitz, whose patience we sorely tried and who nevertheless came up with inspired solutions to every problem. The photo research was begun by Matt Ginella, and the task was completed, often under impossible deadlines, by the peerless Gregory Payan, whose coolness under fire is matched only by his ability to go without sleep. Leslie Falk cheerfully looked after countless small details. Ben McGrath provided early technical support and helped with the text editing. Without all these people this book could never have happened.

Illustration Credits

Pages i, 131, 208, 233, 235: Robert Beck; ii–iii, 2–3, 116 (bottom), 117, 122, 149 (bottom right), 177 (top), 232 (bottom): Bob Martin/*Sports Illustrated*; iv–v: Jim Gund/*Sports Illustrated*; vi, 20 (top), 32, 39, 40, 42, 56, 59, 78, 81, 82, 83, 84–85, 89, 92 (top and bottom), 93, 94–95, 102, 108 (top), 110, 112–13, 169, 190, 198–99, 204, 219, 224, 225 (top), 238: Bettmann/Corbis; vii, 174–75: JoAnn Dost Golf Editions; viii–ix: Fred Vuich/*Sports Illustrated*; x–xi, 53, 120, 172–73, 184–85, 223 (bottom), 234: Tony Roberts; xii–xiii, 118–19, 121 (top right), 149 (bottom left), 164, 167: Jacqueline Duvoisin/*Sports Illustrated*; xiv, 201 (top): David Walberg/*Sports Illustrated*; 1: Ann Dickinson; 9, 124: Simon Bruty/*Sports Illustrated*; 10–11, 24–25, 74–75, 162–63, 244–45: Macduff Everton; 11 (bottom right), 18–19, 44, 64–65, 171, 192, 193 (bottom), 220: Michael Hobbs Golf Collection; 12, 27, 35, 38, 41, 46–47, 159, 170, 194–95: USGA; 14, 15 (bottom): Timepix; 15 (top), 16, 17, 20 (bottom): courtesy of St. Andrews University Library; 21 (bottom), 22, 166, 191, 213, 241: Hulton-Deutsch Collection/Corbis; 21 (top), 147 (bottom): Lane Stewart/*Sports Illustrated*; 23: Mansell/Timepix; 34, 45, 80, 206–7, 221: Underwood & Underwood/Corbis; 36: Minnesota Historical Society/Corbis; 43: the Jones Family/courtesy of Martin Davis; 52, 96, 222: Historic Golf Photos/Ron Watts Collection; 54–55, 156, 218: Maurice Harmon; 57, 58, 61, 62, 63, 68: courtesy of Jeff Ellis/The Clubmaker's Art; 60: courtesy of Bob Pringle/Old Troon Sporting Antiques; 67: Ben Van Hook/*Sports Illustrated*; 69: John Hanlon/*Sports Illustrated*; 69 (bottom): U.S. Patent #3,655,188 owned by Karsten Solheim/Karsten Manufacturing Company; 76–77, 137, 197: John Zimmerman/*Sports Illustrated*; 79: Hy Peskin/Timepix; 86, 88, 94–95, 193 (top), 196: Associated Press; 87: Martin Nathan/Timepix; 90: Ralph Crane/Blackstar; 104: Peter Robinson; 105, 160, 176 (bottom), 179, 186: Larry Lambrecht; 106: Joe McNally/*Sports Illustrated*; 107: Kyodo News Agency; 108 (bottom): Gerry Cranham/*Sports Illustrated*; 111: Kemsley Picture Service; 114, 134–35, 139, 141 (top), 147 (top), 200, 202–3, 232 (top): James Drake/*Sports Illustrated*; 115: Richard A. Cooke/Corbis; 116 (top): Tony Tomsic/*Sports Illustrated*; 121 (top left): Dave Cannon/Getty Images; 121 (bottom left): Gilbert Rossi; 121 (bottom right): John Biever/*Sports Illustrated*; 123: Reuters/Corbis; 128, 246: Dick Durrance; 130: Farrel Grehan/Corbis; 132, 133, 201 (bottom): Leviton-Atlanta/*Sports Illustrated*; 136: Robert Huntzinger/*Sports Illustrated*; 138, 223 (top): Getty Images/MSI; 140 (top), 142: Walter Iooss/*Sports Illustrated*; 141 (bottom): courtesy of IMG; 143: Richard Mackson/*Sports Illustrated*; 144–45, 146, 148, 150–51, 237: John Iacono/*Sports Illustrated*; 149 (top left), 188: Tony Triolo/*Sports Illustrated*; 149 (top right), 205 (bottom left): Eric Schweikhardt/*Sports Illustrated*; 152: Jon Ferrey/Getty Images; 158: European; 161: Graham Finlayson/*Sports Illustrated*; 165: Tony Roberts/Corbis; 168: Edward M. Pio Roda/*Sports Illustrated;* 176 (top): Michael S. Yamashita/Corbis; 177 (bottom): Morton Beebe S.F./Corbis; 178: Tufts Archives; 181, 182: courtesy of Seminole Golf Club; 189: Darren Carroll/*Sports Illustrated*; 205 (top left): courtesy of Martin Davis; 205 (top right): Sheedy & Long/*Sports Illustrated*; 205 (bottom right): Michael O'Byron/*Sports Illustrated*; 211: Gary Kufner/Corbis; 225 (bottom): Harry How/Getty Images; 226: Susan Allen Sigmon; 227: Neil Leifer/*Sports Illustrated*; 228–29 (Nelson swing sequence), 230–31 (Stewart swing sequence): photos provided by *Golf Digest*; 228–29 (Weiskopf swing sequence), 230–31 (Webb swing sequence): Leonard Kamsler; 242: courtesy of Jack Welch.

Index

Rawlins, Horace, 40
Rawls, Betsy, 4, 93, 196
Ray, Ted, 34, 37, 141
Raynor, Seth, 178
Redmond, Jack, 80
Rees, Dai, 112–13
Reid, John, 35, 36, 109
Reilly, Rick, 148
Reinmuth, Dean, 234
Republican National Committee, 50
Reynolds, Jim, 56–57
Rhodes, Teddy, 201
Riviera Country Club (Los Angeles), 51, 103, 178
Road Hole, The (St. Andrews), 161, 187, 193
Roberts, Clifford, 92, 93, 182, 200, 209
Roberts, Oral, 217
Robertson, Allan, 12, 16, 20, 60, 160
Robinson, Jackie, 190
Robinowitz, Bernard, 216
Rodriguez, Chi Chi, 147, 238
Rokko, Mount, golf course at (Kobe, Japan), 106–7
Rosario Golf Club (Argentina), 108
Rosburg, Bob, 137
Rose, Justin, 220
Ross, Alex, 81
Ross, Donald J., 81, 169, 174, 178, 180, 182–83
Royal Aberdeen Golf Course, 23
Royal & Ancient Golf Club of St. Andrews. *See* St. Andrews, Royal & Ancient Golf Club of
Royal Birkdale Golf Course, 108
Royal Bombay Golf Society, The, 109
Royal Calcutta golf course (India), 115
Royal Canadian Golf Association, 110
Royal County Down golf course (Northern Ireland), 161
Royal Dornoch Golf Club, 74, 164
Royal Lytham & St. Annes golf course, 191
Royal St. George''s Golf Club (England), 44, 167
Ruck, Mary Anne, 28

Runyan, Paul, 8, 225
Ruth, Babe, 142, 193
Ryder, Samuel, 114
Ryder Cup, The, 114–16, 120

S

St. Andrews, Old Course at, 4, 14, 16, 18–19, 22, 43, 44, 45, 110, 159, 160, 166–67, 178, 190
St. Andrews, Royal & Ancient Golf Club of (R&A), 14, 15–16, 21, 23, 38, 40, 41, 45, 63, 66, 67, 105, 110
St. Andrews, village of, 12–13
St. Andrews Cathedral, 21
St. Andrew's Golf Club (New York), 34–36, 46–47
St. Andrews Ladies Golf Club, 191
St. Louis Cardinals, 194
Sampson, Curt, 224
Sanders, Doug, 96, 98, 222, 226
Sand Hills Golf Club (Nebraska), 178
Sands, Charles, 40
Sandwich, 42
Saraceni (original name of Gene Sarazen), 42
Sarazen, Gene, 4, 26–27, 42, 63, 83, 93, 194
Savannah Golf Club, 35
Schenkel, Chris, 136, 137
Schofield, Ken, 234
Scott, Adam, 221
Scott, Lady Margaret, 23, 192
Secretariat, 8
Seminole golf gourse (Palm Beach, Florida), 103, 180, 182
Seton (site of golf game of Mary, Queen of Scots), 14
Shadow Creek Golf Club, 170
Shady Rest country club, 206–7
Sharkey, Hal, 82
Shell's Wonderful World of Golf, 138
Sherwood Oaks Country Club (California), 170
Shinnecock Hills Golf Club, 38, 191
Shippen, John, 191, 204
Shoal Creek Country Club (Alabama), 209
Sifford, Charlie, 201, 204

Silver King SW1 (ball), 58
Singh, Vijay, 109, 116–17
Siwanoy Country Club (Mt. Vernon, New York), 81
Smith, Alex, 41, 43
Smith, Horton, 93
Smith, Mike, 127
Smith, Rick, 234
Smith, Sydney, 137
Smondrowski, Joe, 125, 127
Snead, Samuel Jackson (Slamming Sammy), 78–80, 81, 83, 86, 88, 91, 96, 103, 107, 122–23, 138, 153
Solheim, Karsten, 57–59, 66, 69
Solheim Cup, 120
Sorenstam, Annika, 105, 122, 210
South Carolina Golf Club (Charleston), 35
Southern Hills (Tulsa), 103, 178, 217
Spalding, A. G. & Brothers, 41, 61, 170
Spaulding's Rob't. T. Jones five-iron, 62
Star Challenger, The (ball), 58
Stark, John, 4, 73–75
Stewart, Payne, 230–31
Stirk, David, 62
Stirling, Alexa, 192
Stoddard, Laurence, 38
Stranahan, Frank, 91, 92
Strange, Curtis, 146
Suggs, Louise, 82, 196
Sugihara, Teruo, 106–7, 124
Sunningdale Golf Club (Berkshire, England), 166, 192
Super Harlequin (ball), 58
Swinley Forest golf course, 166

T

Tait, Freddie, 29
Tam O'Shanter Country Club, 136, 200
Tatum, Sandy, 67
Taylor, John Henry (J. H.), 26–27, 41
Texas Open, 81
Thomas, George C., Jr., 52, 178
Thomas, Stanley, 178
Thomas E. Wilson Company, 41
Thompson, Hall, 209